The
Battle for
Control
within
Relationships

Dr. Isaac O'Quin

ISBN: 978-1-954095-96-0
The Battle for Control Within Relationships

For permission requests, write to the publisher at the address below.

Yorkshire Publishing
1425 E 41st Pl
Tulsa, OK 74105
www.YorkshirePublishing.com
918.394.2665

Published in the USA

The
Battle for Control
within
Relationships

Section I

THE DEVIOUS BEHAVIOR
OF CON-WOMEN

Section II

THE CRIMINAL MIND
OF CORRUPT MEN

Dr. Isaac O'Quin

TULSA

Author's Preface

The idea of writing this book came to me one afternoon after a counseling session with a married couple. I've worked with many couples in the past and continue to do so today. However, working with this couple for more than a year made me think about writing this book. I am never surprised at the things I hear concerning problems between couples, yet they continue to repeat themselves over and over, again and again. Many of them fail to see the bigger picture of what is really going on with their relationship.

Making poor decisions in finding the right mate between men and women has become the key issue because of the lack of understanding about each other's role. The book contains two sections, (Section 1 for men and Section 2 for women) concerning the initial behavior and conduct of both males and females when looking for companionship. The goal of this book is to help the reader see what is truly happening before getting involved and after getting involved in a relationship. The book is speaking to readers at their level of how they see each other before and after getting involved. It will help them see their failures and downfalls should they continue ignoring the signs.

There are a few solutions that are being shared in the book. However, the idea is to get the reader to want more help in understanding the right way to live as a couple. The book does not give solutions to every problem but, instead, helps them see the broader picture of what is truly going on in their relationship.

Part of the ongoing problem many couples face is not having a good foundation of truth to balance their lives. Their souls are not harmonizing as one in order to be on the same wavelength of life. There are solutions to any and every kind of problem that occurs in life. However, without a true foundation to stand on, regardless of how good a solution may be, it will only work temporarily. People in a relationship will never find true fulfillment in life until they have accepted the Creator of the foundation of life.

I put a lot of Scripture into the first book, which I wrote in 2005 and published in 2007. My goal then was to guide people toward answers to many of the struggles they were facing in life. This book, however, will use a different method of helping people see the bigger picture of what is really happening within themselves. My writing will hopefully open their eyes to the reality of life and help; them to understand the environment they are engaged in. I will drop down to their level of language understanding: How they see each other, how they engage with each other, how they think and operate when they are together, their attitudes and their personalities along with their conniving behaviors.

There will be Bible verses here and there, with chapter

locations. However, my aim is to share the good news by allowing them to see what life is like without a solid foundation of truth through Jesus Christ. I am hoping to draw the reader's attention to wanting more then what this world has to offer as solutions to their problems. Please take note: Throughout this book, you will notice I did not capitalize the first letter of "satan." For an angel who wanted to be above God, who created him, it does not make sense; to give him the same capital recognition as our God, who created all things. I choose not to acknowledge him, even to the point of violating grammatical rules.

Introduction

I have seen many relationships fall through the cracks due to false intellectual behaviors. My work as a counselor has enabled me to see clear through the small talk when people are trying to impress me with their antics. My goal for this book is to open your eyes to the real person you may be getting involved with. It will help you stay alert when your partner thinks your guard is down. My main focus for the first half of this book will be: "THE DEVIOUS BEHAVIOR OF CON-WOMEN." Later I will address the other side of this coin by revealing: "THE CRIMINAL MIND OF CORRUPT MEN" in Section II.

I want to commend all of the good women and men who have maintained a positive level of intelligent behavior and truthfulness throughout their relationship; before marriage and after marriage. It is important to note that this book is not gang-banging on all women and men or women and men in premarital relationships. It is merely showing the dark side of the population that does not hold true morals and values over a long-term period. The society we live in today is far different from the society of fifty to one hundred years ago. Many parents during that time put a great deal of emphasis on teaching their young girls how they should respect themselves before dating. Many also learned from their mothers how they should treat their husbands by watching how their father was treated.

Today's society presents a different culture for young women, it is producing women who are more independent and like being in charge. Much of this behavior stems from the women's rights movement during its early years. Women have had to struggle to take care of children when deadbeat dads were not around to support them. We have seen a great deal of this and other negative behaviors from men that have changed the behavior of women. However, there are still a lot of good men in the world, men who desire a woman with good morals and values on how they should treat a man, especially when they are doing the right thing.

This book will help men learn to be more patient when they are being tempted the most, in the early parts of their relationship. Patience will help wear down the false behaviors of the woman who is not being her real self. You will know if it is true love or if you are being targeted for your wealth or popularity in society. There could be many other reasons for women wanting to get involved with men besides what is mentioned above. However, the real goal for you men will be to stay focused on what it is you are looking for in a good woman.

Ladies, my advice to you in looking for a good man will be to check his background and get to know as much about him as possible. These are not the days of yesteryear, when a man showed the respect needed to begin building a relationship that would last. Good women are being murdered every day by men who have no foundation of value or truth to live by. Good women need to stop rushing themselves into relationships that end up in bed on the first date. I will do my best to open your eyes to the dangers that await you in this world. You will be informed of the many types of behaviors that men have and how they see you as a woman. You will know when it's the right time to move forward or to close the door to strange behaviors.

However, as you get deeper into the reading of this book, you will discover a great deal more about yourself and your partner. You will find that my writing is simple and down to earth; I do not beat around the bush nor do I bite my tongue about what I have to say (only when I'm eating). My goal is to open your eyes to the real truth and what is really happening within your relationship. Hopefully, you will be able to laugh at what is not affecting you. But instead help someone you know who is being mistreated or misled from the situations you see in this book.

CONTENTS

SECTION II

THE CRIMINAL MIND
OF CORRUPT MEN

Section I

THE DEVIOUS BEHAVIOR OF CON-WOMEN

Chapter 1

FISHING FOR A GOOD MAN

It has been said that men and women are like fish in the sea. You don't have to be a good fisherwoman to catch a good-looking or a healthy-looking man; you just need to have the right tools and know-how. Women have become very smart with the techniques they use to catch men. Unlike the early years of dating, women are not falling for that sweet talk or the big promises some men make during the dating period. They want proof and a closer examination of what lies behind all the sweet talk and quick moves. For many years I have seen the premeditated behaviors of women before marriage vows; then, shortly after the settling down, it begins to unfold. Once the ring is on and the door is locked, that poor soul of a man has no idea what will be brewing inside that woman over the next twelve to twenty-four months.

Women have uncovered a great deal of strength about themselves. I'm not talking physical strength; it's more mental and psychological controlling. They have learned to use their femininity, along with lies, to get what they want; that's why so many men are in jail today. Women know that the courts and the police officers will side with them if they look helpless enough. If they really want to hurt the guy or put him away for a long time, all they have to say is: he hit me or he raped me or he tried to rape one of the children, then there goes the neighborhood. The man in just about all cases will lose the battle because he's a male.

Men in the Middle East know all too well about the danger of letting their women have the same freedom as they do. They know how weak-minded they are when they see the legs on a woman or her chest with part of a breast showing. They can't seem to get those images out of their head, so they make their women cover up from head to toe and they take away the majority of their rights. Unlike here in America, where a woman can walk around stark naked and dare anyone to mess with her. That, my friend, is the kind of seducing and controlling power that can drive a man crazy with lust and can get you in big trouble if you try to sample the goods without permission. The women here in America know they can have it both ways because they know the law is on their side.

Some women can be very analytical when questioning a man whom they may be interested in and that's great, if she is being truthful. However, others may be looking for a guy who will roll over and bark every time he sees a part of her that turns him on. That's the weakness that many men have in our society today. A woman who desires to be in control throughout most of the relationship will seek this type of man. She knows how to tease and make him beg for what she knows he enjoys the most. I have shared with many men the fact that you never fully get to know a woman even after you marry her. Women are like bullfrogs and butterflies when it comes to changes in their lives. You never know what she's going to be from one day to the next, a bullfrog or a butterfly.

The downside to that is that you will never win either way. If she becomes a bullfrog, she's bullying you all day and making your life so miserable that you wish she would disappear. However, you would think that a butterfly would be the ideal wife to be around; don't bet on it, my friend. Remember the saying of Mohammed Ali before he went into the ring to fight: "Float like a butterfly and sting like a bee." That is what happens when that woman is being nice to you; she wants something from you that may cost you a lot of money or hard work on your part. If you do not give in to those demands, you can kiss that butterfly goodbye after a period of time. No more being nice to you for days on end until you nut up with the goods or with what she wants you to do for her.

A strong-minded woman will look for men in areas that depict much of their behavior, therefore giving them the edge concerning the type of control they will have in the relationship. Of course, I have to say some men are just downright losers because of the way many of them think when they see a decent-looking woman. They let their tongue hang out and their pants tighten up with lust just looking at her. If the poor soul has a good job and or is well educated with a good income, he would be the kind of target this strong-minded woman is looking for.

If Samson from the early Bible days could be here today, he would tell you upfront that you can't think with your tongue hanging out and your pants all tightened up. He of all men knew the downfall from this behavior and how it betrayed him to his death. However, do you think Delilah felt sorry for him when they came and took him to the dungeon? On the contrary, she was paid a handsome ransom for betraying him. She, like many of the women I am referring to, was no different than the way she operated during that period. So, men, I have to say, be careful of your weak-minded behaviors, you may end up losing everything; as so many have already done.

Being among the right group of people to associate with also plays a big role in selecting the kind of man she is looking for. It would also depend on the clientele of the group of people she will be part of. She will adorn herself with the right kind of clothes and makeup to make a big impression on the one who gives her the most attention. She will then parade herself around as though she is lost or is waiting for someone. However, that someone will be the first sucker who is attracted to her troubling look with a desire to get to know her while his tongue is hanging out. Many of these women are not so much as looking for the most handsome guy; the guy could look like a monster from the black lagoon, as long as he has what she's looking for he would do just fine. Unlike most men who are looking for Miss Universe in looks, many women just want the bottom line of what they could get from the relationship.

Once the prey has been trapped and he's showing concerns about her being all alone, she kicks her thinking process into second gear. To the man, she looks like the most intelligent woman among the group, as she struts about looking innocent and lost. However, her goal is to analyze his every move, conversation, attitude, and behavior. She will either let herself get to know him, based on his conversation and how well he articulates himself, or pretend she is already with someone. These are the key factors that will allow her to continue moving forward, or at some point stop him in his tracks.

The average woman who really wants to do well by her man seems to do just the contrary of the women who are out to rule and control. Many of them seem to be naïve about what they should be looking for in a man. They tend to gravitate to men who are abusive and are of a no-good nature toward women. Although I feel there should be a balance for all women in selecting the right man for their mate, that may never be the case. I will be addressing this issue more in my next book about the behavior of men toward women.

Chapter 2

USING THE RIGHT BAIT

M ost men are attracted to women with long hair or hairstyles that make them stand out from other women. The softness of a woman is what most men enjoy the most: being able to rub against her face, kiss her lips, and nibble her neck and shoulder. However, that can be hard to do if the woman is wearing tons of makeup, which can be a big turn-off for some men. For me, I have always been fascinated with the natural look of a woman without makeup all over her face. I think her real beauty causes her in most cases to be her real self. However, many women seem to have low self-esteem about the natural way they look and feel they have to add to themselves cosmetics to compete with other women.

What men fail to understand is that the cosmetics that a woman wears about her face do not tell you everything about her; the woman can be mesmerizing to a man until he gets to know her fully. In many cases, some of these women will pretend to be more than they appear to be. The goal is to impress you by arranging in their minds the right intellectual behavior to use with the kind of makeup that's on their face. It's like wearing a mask; you become whatever face you put on and, if you don't act it out, you are not the person you appear to be. Most women who conduct themselves this way will find it hard later to find the right runway to land on. In other words, as the relationship builds to a higher level with their mate, at some point they will get tired of being the person that they never were. That is when the real Mr. Jekyll comes out.

I have always been captivated by women who wear dresses. To me, it makes them look like the women that they really are: someone a man would love to hold in his arms and look at after a hard day's work. However, most women don't feel like being women, they want to play both sides of the fence and yet have the rights of a woman. Well, you might ask what that means. It means most women today are dressing in competition with the man. They wear pantsuits, hard shoes, tennis shoes, and blue jeans, and are involved in many of the hard sports that men are in. Many of them want to make it clear that they only need a man for certain things, such as security, income needs, social life when they choose to have one, or someone they can control to fit their needs.

Those are just some of their needs; I'm sure there are many more that I have not listed. However, the women who hold these values don't fully understand that the average man is looking for a woman to satisfy him at his greatest hour of need. The average man is looking for more than just a female partner; for the most part, he wants someone who will satisfy his sexual needs for the long haul. Everything else will fall into place as long as she is taking care of his most intimate needs. However, these are the kind of men that some women see as being weak and easy to control.

They will appear to you in the most attractive ways, causing you to eat your heart out just to have one night along with her. However, most intelligent men will be submissive to her desires and are willing to wait for the right opportunity before moving forward.

I call these kinds of women slow killers of good-hearted men who truly want to do right. We all have been suckered into what we thought was a good thing only to find out later that we had been taken for a ride. Women with undercover agendas toward men can be very clever in how they operate. They are like meat-eating plants; they adorn themselves with the sweetest smelling fragrant and will wear their best attire. The first fly that smells and sees this beautiful plant heads straight for the opening, only to get stuck and totally disabled. That's why it is so important for men to think before allowing themselves to be controlled by their lustful eyes. Once the poor soul begins to nibble on this sweet-smelling irresistible mountain of clay, his mind becomes locked on one thing. Her soft feminine voice, rolling eyes, and juicy lips seem to paralyze him as he tries to move away but can't. He becomes hypnotized and forgets the man that he really was before her spell.

This kind of woman sets many types of traps that will snare even the most intelligent men. It is said that with a grain of faith we can move mountains that others would think is impossible to do. However, with some women in our world, all they have to do is stand in the right place and the mountains will come to them. Men who have built empires for themselves are taken down by a simple, soft-spoken, Jezebel-looking woman who has knocked them on their butts. Think about it; look at the prisons in our society today and in the past. They are filled mostly with what gender? That's right, men, men who were once brilliant in many ways, but allowed that a seducing Jezebel of a woman brings them down to their knees.

As funny as it may be, we all have our needs and weaknesses but most of us men seem to become the prey most of the time. That's because we're too smart for our own good and clumsy most of the time. CLUMSY, what do you mean by that, you might ask. Well, look at yourself and ask yourself what would you do if you were being watched by a honeycomb of a woman and all you could think about is her eyes on you as you imagine her being in your arms. Then you hear this song going off in your head; don't.... fight it surrender.... to the Peter Paul almond cluster. As you hear yourself giving in to this mountain of lust, you slowly find yourself walking over to find out what it's all about. Once you introduce yourself and hear her soft, sweet-sounding feminine voice say "Hi".... your force field becomes penetrated and you are now putty in her hands.

It would take a strong mind to resist the temptations of the Jezebels in our world today. More and more women are disguising themselves as being what they are truly not and are ruining the lives of good men. These are men who really want to do well and have a good showing of themselves in society. They instead let the Delilahs of our world betray them and have them sent to the dungeons while they feast off your successful years of hard work and the accumulation of wealth. I know for a fact that some of you men who are reading are dealing with these kinds of issues right now. You are wondering to yourself: How do I deal with it now or how do I get out of this mess? These are good questions and the answers are easy. If you're not married to her, you should stop and analyze your situation and find out if the woman you're with is the same woman you met. Remember the makeup mask and the intellectual behavior that came from that mask: Is it still the same or has it all changed? Without knowing it, many men forget the original woman they first met after a long period of time. They become blinded about who she really was and continue to deal with the behavior of who she continues to be today.

However, if you are married to this kind of woman and your eyes are now open as to what you remember about her when you first met, talk to her about it. If you find it difficult getting her to stop the negative behavior toward you, seek marriage counseling. It is the best solution for your current situation and in most cases can be very helpful. There is nothing that says a bad woman cannot be changed; it would, however, take patience on your part for that to come about. There is good in all of us; that is, if we choose to do well toward others.

Being careful of what you say and how you say it contains the locking key for many women. They could pin you to the mat without you knowing it. Many men become hypnotized when hearing the right words that make them feel unique compared to all other men. Several things are taking place as this behavior continues: **(1)** she is stimulating your actions in a controlling way, (2) she motivates how you see yourself, and (3) she is reducing you down to a childlike submissive person.

People who are in prison find it very difficult to meet their intimate needs. This is because the opposite sex is not housed in the same location. Therefore, many of them are stimulated by the way they look at each other, based on the size, appearance, and intelligence of the person. Many are forced into doing things they have no desire of doing with the same sex. However, some know it's just a matter of time before it happens to them. In most cases, they make up their mind to take charge by befriending the aggressor to get favors. It then becomes a two-sided street for the prey; he/she gets their needs met and the predator is satisfied with not having to fight to get what he/she wants. Isn't that the behavior of the women I am speaking about in this book? For the most part, they know they can never beat you physically, so they use the right words to keep things under control.

Those who raise children know all too well how to get them involved in things we feel would be good for them. If it's music, arts, dance, or just wanting them to be a good kid, we say the right things to encourage them to continue in their effort of doing good. Of course, there are the rewards we give out to help stimulate the process; these, in turn, motivate their ongoing actions. However, all of this may sound simple and easy but in many cases, it's not. Some parents can be very forceful and demanding and create consequences when they can't get what they want out of their children. This is the same approach some women use with their husbands or boyfriends to get them motivated in the right direction by catering to their personal needs and not theirs.

It has been said that international prisoners can sometimes be beaten down and deprived of food and drink each day. This torture is used to make the prisoner give information about their country or those whom they are involved with. It does have its breaking points because a person can take only so much of this type of abuse over a period of time; but when they become submissive to the torturer, they are rewarded with personal needs. This pattern of behavior is closely related to the women I am speaking of in this book. They may not use physical torture to get their men to submit to their will, however, they do use tactics that deprive them of their benevolent needs. In turn, it creates a submissive behavior on the part of the man to do whatever it takes to get his personal needs met. It is hard for some men to see the big picture of what is happening around them. Some women can cause a man to develop tunnel vision and not see anything that she's doing to them, only what she wants them to see. Over time these men find themselves knee-deep in debt or with promises hard for them to maintain.

Chapter 3

REELING IN THE BIG CATCH

Understanding his likes and dislikes plays a big role in maintaining control of the man. Women who use these tactics are very clever in how they manipulate getting their needs met, while at the same time keeping him at bay when he's not needed. It has been said that women have a greater need for love and affection than men but I don't buy that for all. However, from what I have seen and have experienced in life working with clients, most men tend to need more love and affection than most women. Women may be sensitive in feeling the need to be told how much they are loved and appreciated but men seem to have the greater need overall. Many women go through life not having a desire to be intimate with a man nor showing a desire for affection from a man. But, on the other hand, a man who is fully functional and wants to be satisfied by a woman has a greater need in many different ways.

A man's world is controlled by several elements that will keep him calm and at bay when being with a woman of his choice: (1) Seeing what he wants, (2) being able to touch and feel what he enjoys, (3) enjoying the smell of the woman, and (4) tasting the elements of the world he comes to know. Women who fail to see these elements in a

the wild are the same way, I believe it is a natural instinct for the male to act this way when mating or just fooling around. For the dominating woman, this becomes another tool in her arsenal of control. However, not all women understand what they have under their control. Those who do understand expand their imagination in utilizing these tools to their greater advantage. The weaker vessel seems to always win over the stronger vessel after strong observation of his behavior is shown. Men who show their cards to the opposite player find themselves at a disadvantage before the game is over. When she sees what you have and don't have, it opens the door for new tricks to be played on you. The man who thought he had it under control, but instead was being controlled, may have ended up taking a cold shower in the end.

The internet has opened up all kinds of ways to check people out and do background checks. This in and of itself has given women the tools to protect themselves from predators who feed on them. However, this same tool gives them the opportunity to find good-behaving men who are trying to do well in society. Having said that; the shoe is now on the other foot as the predator. Women who prey on men now have the advantage of what to look for when wanting to be in control. Most men will not go online to do background checks on women. They tend to make decisions with their eyes, their thoughts, their lustful desires, and their mouth. Many are too busy trying to be smooth talkers rather than good thinkers.

Men who pull the apple from the tree without examining it will bite into it only to find it has a large worm inside, with half of it in their mouth. Trying to spit it out doesn't do any good because the taste is already on the inside. Your mind is now locked on the awful-tasting worm, which you can't seem to shake. This is what happens when men get trapped in relationships with controlling women. They want to leave but can't, they want to stop being nice but can't, and they want to find a nicer woman but can't. The reason that many can't just walk away is that the controlling woman knows their weakness. She knows how to make them feel good in bed and she knows how to give them exactly what they want. All of this while at the same time being mean and hateful throughout the relationship and getting exactly what she wants when she wants it. The poor man will be on a seesaw over good loving and being abused at different times.

Many women are not computer-savvy; their analyzing depends on many of the comments from their girlfriends concerning their choice of a good man. However, this still does not stop their false behaviors in dating good men. In fact, it amplifies them in other ways because friends can be very helpful in sharing information. Some women rely on other women who have many male friends, in the hope of getting to know them based on the knowledge they have. Having female friends like this creates a powerhouse of knowledge and personal information about men they may hope to meet. Picking the brain of a girlfriend about her male friends is as good as or, in some cases, better than using a computer.

Current direct knowledge of anything or anyone gives a person the edge in moving forward with whatever their plans are. I myself, like many men, have more female friends than male friends. However, some women have many female friends as well as male friends, which gives them a greater advantage of knowledge about the people they know. We often hear the phrase "knowledge is power"; well, it certainly is in this case. A woman who has ill intentions of taking advantage of a good thing will go through hoops and hurdles to make sure it is the right fish to catch. The knowledge obtained from friends about her catch ensures that she is truly on the right track for achieving her goal.

Chapter 4

EXAMINING THE PRIZE
WITH CAREFUL EYES

Once the fish is caught and in sight, in hand, and in touch for examination, she goes into Stella mode. She will present herself in many ways as a successful woman to impress him into liking her while, on the other hand, analyzing his comments about her. This small talk is more of an appetizer in preparation for the most important questions to come. Questions relating to his background and lifestyle. A woman who is motivated and well informed about the man she is enticing will study his response very closely. She will more likely take note of his reaction to whatever she says to him and how he addresses the issues. This will let her know whether to wait for a later time to dig into his background or to move forward; that is, if she feels comfortable enough to do so at that time. The information obtained from friends would still not be enough to decide to move forward. Over time, she would have to do some deep study in understanding his behavior and attitude and how he reacts to negativity. Of course, this should be the same desire for every woman seeking a good man. But women who are out looking for a man to be their slave have different intentions of how they plan to spend time and please that man.

I would say that most men are intelligent enough to know when most women are being real about themselves. However, there are a lot of women who are very good at playing the dating game and fooling the very elite group of men. This type of woman is extra careful not to make the wrong choice in her selection of men. To choose a man with the same intentions as herself would be like two freight engines running into each other. A strong-minded man will not tolerate such behavior from a woman who wants to make him her slave. Some women have ended up being raped, beaten, and even killed for treating a man with such low levels of respect. It can be hard to tease some men with sex and then turn around and back away if he doesn't bow to her desires. This is why a woman of this caliber will take her time and may go through half a dozen or more men before making her choice.

Most women enjoy eating chocolate of many different shapes, flavors, and sizes from a candy box loaded with all sorts of those goodies. However, when a good man is trying to build a strong relationship and bond with a woman he hardly knows, she too can be like one of the candies in the box he's giving her. You never know what you're gonna get until it's too late. There's the smooth chocolate, the nutty, the caramel, the coconut, and so on. The thing the guy should hope for is that she will not turn out to be like one of the candies in the box. They all could turn out to be bad for him either way. If she's too smooth, she could trap you like Delilah did Samson; too nutty, she'll drive you crazy; too much caramel, you'll get stuck and can't get out; and if she's the chocolate coconut, she will choke you to death. I am speaking to you metaphorically, in the hope that you can read between the line of what I'm saying.

Most women (if not all) can become unpredictable at certain times in their lives. Unlike men with facial hair and age growth, women deal with female changes of the body, periods, and hormones (as do men as well) changes. The difference is that some women, regardless of these changes, can maintain control of who they are and who they want to be. They understand these changes and have determined how they plan to treat their man. This could be good or bad; that's why it's so hard for good men to find Miss Right. Miss Evil can look like Miss Good; however, some telltale signs will let you know what she's up to. That is if you are not as weak as a dishrag from her spell over you. Once she has figured you out in every way, your weakness, your likes and dislikes, your habits, your play times, your behaviors, and the kind of lovemaking you truly enjoy, it then becomes time to train you. Well, you might ask, "Train me in what?" Good question, my friends; getting you ready for how she plans to control you. It may be months and more likely years before your eyes are truly open to what is really happening to you.

When you look back in time and remember how it all got started, you will realize that it began later with questions concerning your background in an intense way. Yet it was smooth and done in a precise way without you getting offended. She had all the right questions to ask in order to make her final decision on whether to settle with you as a mate. Some of you may remember how her kind and loving behavior continued for months and possibly years before the changes started taking place. However, you being as nice and respectful as you thought you could be in the beginning; did not ask the kind of background questions about her as she did about you.

Even if you did, you found those questions not answered, but switched to a different topic, causing you to forget the original question you asked. The conversation would get so polluted with other small talk that your mind would get swayed away from getting to know more about her background and lifestyle behaviors. This is where many of you fall between the cracks. She now knows all about you and your background but you failed to gather the information you needed to help you make a sensible decision. Had you known what her background relationships were like, you then could have made a better decision about moving forward with her or letting her go for a better catch.

A woman like this knows how much information she is willing to share with you. However, she will only tell you what she wants you to know about herself. If she came from a prior bad relationship, she will only tell you about how bad and mean he was and not about what she was doing in creating the breakup. She's looking for sympathy from you and hoping that you will see her as Miss Goody Two-Shoes that could do no wrong. This kind of woman knows how to distract you during conversations and questions she doesn't want to answer. Think about it, guys: As you are sitting in front of this beautiful molten lava, lust in the eyes of a woman, you find yourself mesmerized by her looks and body parts. It is no wonder that so many good men fall between the cracks; they can't seem to control their thoughts. In my mind, "Delilah" is the epitome of every conniving woman who is up to no good in a man's life.

Chapter 5

MAINTAINING A TIGHT
GRIP ON THE CATCH

Many women like this will have many male friends on the sideline and some may have been or may still be intimate with some of them. Of course, you won't know this until you have been fully acclimated to her lifestyle and the way she associates with other people. Months and years may go by and you may never know the real truth about the men she is associating with. You may see them periodically on different occasions, thinking this is someone she got to know during the time you two have been together. However, your thinking will be far from the truth; while you're thinking she's out with her girlfriends, she's out with her sidekick, her other boyfriend, the one you met at a social gathering, thinking he is someone you both met for the first time. Whether she's your girlfriend or your wife; the game is still played the same way. The big difference is: WHO'S CHILDREN ARE YOU RAISING? Many men become oblivious to what is really happening before their eyes. They become so mesmerized with how she makes them feel in bed that they can only think of the next night filled with more pleasurable moments. She's got you hooked like the ring in a bull's nose and, not only that, she might have you working two jobs just to satisfy her wants and needs.

For both partners to have a decent and successful lifestyle, it would (in most cases) require both partners to work full-time jobs, especially for hungry women who are never satisfied with what they already have. The problem with both parties working is this: Some women think that in a marriage they shouldn't have to use their money to take care of anything. They feel that the man should use all his money to take care of them and everything that needs to be done to make life good for the both of them while she uses her money to splurge about, acting as though she's rich and living a lifestyle beyond most women. Many good men find themselves in this situation and believe that it is okay. Older men from generations back were taught that this is how the man should operate when taking care of his wife and children. However, today's society is demanding more from couples and families.

The man who works two jobs to support a woman who is also working and is getting no help from her (in my opinion) is downright dumb and stupid. No man should become a slave to any woman, regardless of how good she may be in bed. If you can't see what is happening around you and between you and her, you will begin to age more rapidly as you worry about ways of making her happier being with you. However, let's look at the other side of that coin: What if she's not making you as happy as you would like to be? Yet you truly love her, even though she treats you like a dog. She holds back on being nice to you in bed because you want to buy or give her what she wants. She yells and screams at you (this is called a temper tantrum) during a disagreement. When she does help you take care of any major bills in the house, she tells everyone you're using her for money while at the same time you're working two jobs or doing a lot of overtime on your current job just to satisfy her demands for the lifestyle she wants to live.

No matter what you do in trying to make this woman happy, you will still come out with the short end of the stick. Why? Because your eyes are shut and blinded with love and wanting to stay together; yet, you're not getting back the same kind of love that you are giving. It has taken some men years to wake up from this type of behavior. The Bible says: "For the love of money is the root of all evil." For some people, money becomes their god and love becomes a secondary element to money. For many sensible people, love conquers all things: good, evil, hate, money, revenge, poverty, and wealth.

Regardless of what you may be going through; love will open your eyes to the real truth. It will enable you to take the right steps to correct whatever is going on in your life. How? you might say? The Bible tells us to "first seek ye the Kingdom of Heaven, and all these things shall be added unto you." What things? The things you desire in life. God will also open your eyes to His truth of what is really happening to you in any relationship. Men, don't let a woman become the god in your life. Do not worship what God has created for His purpose; you will truly become blinded and fall into a pit.

Some of the women I am referring to in this book like

to be in the spotlight, showing off to their girlfriends all the fine things they have, such as the big house, the luxury car, fine jewelry, and clothing. Meanwhile, the man who's making all this happen is behind the scenes working his butt off and getting no satisfaction from the person he's doing it for. For those of you who are reading this book, take your blinders off and see for yourselves what state of mind you're in. Only then will you see the big picture of what is really happing in your relationship. A woman who does not respect the man she's with does not deserve to be with him. I know women who, in public places, will greatly disrespect their husband or boyfriend and not think anything of it. In some cases, it's because they have them wrapped around their finger. She will say jump, he will ask how high; she'll say fetch me, he'll say what do you want; and the reward they get in return is a smile, a pat on the head, and a bowl of water with food next to it. I'm speaking metaphorically, but you might say, "Naw, man, that's not me, I'm not that blind."

I've been a professional counselor for 40-plus years, I have worked with women who have been physically, verbally, and sexually abused, and many of them have said: I thought I deserved what happened to me because he told me it was my fault. They were made to believe that a woman is supposed to do what she is told, good or bad. There are good men out there who become weak-minded when it comes to women they melt for. Make no mistake, guys, some of you are really being abused for your kind-hearted behavior. When she sees that you are no more than putty in her hands, she may think she has psychological power in controlling you.

Guys, go back to some of the earlier chapters in this book that talk about the tools a woman uses to catch a good man. Instead of thinking intelligently when meeting her, you're using your eyes full of lust, the blood rushing to the center part of your legs, the hungry sex thoughts popping up in your head, and your tongue dripping for a taste of the goods. Only the power of God can block out such lustful thoughts and help you focus on seeing the big picture for what it is. In today's society, the spotlight woman wants to be in total control. If she can't have it her way, you will reap fewer benefits in the relationship.

Chapter 6

DETERMINING THE RIGHT PLACE
FOR CLOSER EXAMINATION

Women who take part in this devious type of behavior spend a great deal of time practicing how to conduct themselves. They are very clever about using the right words, being on their best behavior, showing a positive attitude, and looking like Jezebel from head to toe. That's the hook that is used to lure you and reel you in. The big question is: Does she like what's in front of her? If she does, she would hope that he will ask her out on a date. Of course, a restaurant would be the ideal place where she could do a closer examination. However, if that does not pan out, then she would have to make do, wherever she agrees to go with him. Once a location has been agreed on, the next step would be to practice her response to certain questions on the first date. Her goal would be to dazzle him even more at the next meeting. She would do this by wearing provocative clothing that will cause his jaw to drop. This, in turn, would cause him to want her even more. Although that would be her goal, she would also play hard to get, causing him to open up about himself to get a second date. The whole process is to keep his mouth drooling over her and wanting to be with her even more.

Now, if that's not enough, she may decide to stall him after he asks for a second date. How? By making it seems like she has a busy schedule and may not have time for a second date. She may instead tell him, "I will call you to let you know if I am open on the date you are requesting," even knowing right there that she has all the time in the world and may not be involved in anything that could cause her to be so busy. The whole purpose of this is to keep you on the hook because you are trying to get your feet more inside her door. As the first meeting continues, she will listen to you more in conversations by agreeing with you on certain issues and disagreeing on issues she doesn't approve of. She will do this with laughter, kindness, and respect for your views throughout.

This back-and-forth behavior will continue until she feels assured that he's the one. She knows all too well that the wrong man knowing what she's up to can physically hurt her really bad and possibly put her in the hospital or in the ground. A woman who shows this type of behavior did not have a good upbringing. Her mother may have done the same thing with her dad and the cycle may have repeated itself over and over with different men while growing up. People often practice what they see and experience as children growing up. Some can break the cycle of sinful behavior through knowledge and understanding as life goes on. However, many chose to follow the path of unrighteousness; they may see the benefits for themselves in other ways from what they saw while growing up with their parents. One will never know when the backlash of their wrongdoing will kick in. Every deed we do in life (good or bad) will come back to bite us somewhere down the line.

The game she plays with men can be compared to Russian roulette: A round cylinder with six holes and one live bullet in one of the chambers. She's hoping that the bullet in the chamber will never get in front of the trigger as she turns him about. As bad as this woman may be, she should not have to suffer from the hands of an angry man due to her devious sinful ways. I do not condone such type of behavior by any woman but I do hope that her sins be forgiven by the one she's offending. However, just the contrary takes place throughout this country and in other parts of the world. Women are disappearing in record numbers and are never found and they are not all bad women. Guys, you must ask yourself: Is revenge the answer for your anger? I would say no, no, no. You must first look at yourself and how you were hoping to take advantage of her because of how she caused you to lust after her. You too are not without the sinful thoughts that came into your head. Forgiving, walking away, and not looking back would be the best solution.

Chapter 7

BEING CAREFUL NOT TO OVERCOOK

T he process will continue as long as you are showing signs of being interested in her. You may have
thought the initial introduction of meeting her
for the first time; was exciting. But then the first date opens
your eyes and your mouth with a WOW. She now has you
on a tootsie roll, nice, sweet and chewy. You are now willing to do whatever it takes to get some of that excitement.
As the first date comes to a close, you find yourself hoping
that she will give you a call later during the week to inform
you about the second date you requested. If you came in
two different cars, you walk her over to her car, hoping to
get a big juicy kiss; instead, you get a big smile, a slight hug,
and a handshake. A far cry from a tight body hug, the kind
that would allow you to feel many of the body parts close
up instead, causing you to go home to have wet dreams.

Now she has you in the mindset of planning and looking forward to the next hopeful date; that is, if she calls
you. You become partially paralyzed by her smell, looks,
shape, and smile. Instead of thinking of more questions to
ask and learning more about her background, you become
lust blinded with hormones in overdrive. I am speaking
to the guys who communicate with their lustful hormones
and can't seem to think clearly. I have counseled men who

have shared with me the big mistakes they have made in selecting women with a high sex appeal about them. They claim she made them feel like they were the right guy when, in essence, they were being bamboozled in every way, until their pockets and wallets were emptied or someone tipped them off as to what was really going on in the relationship. Those guys learned a hard lesson about not doing their homework when getting to know a woman. Many of them got out in time; however, there were quite a few who suffered great hardships. I tell you a truth: It is not good to make decisions based on your lustful hormones.

This kind of woman is very careful not to overcook what she's doing to you. She knows just how much salt and pepper to mix in to keep things spicy and the right amount of sweet sugar in other areas to keep you coming back for more. Sounds like a mousetrap, with you being the mouse. Don't get upset, guys, if you know the shoes you're wearing fit fine but are costing you a lot of money to keep them clean; change them.

Why hang on to something you know you can't afford to maintain? It's like persuading yourself to believe something you know is not true. A self-centered woman shows no mercy toward the people she uses, especially the man she's with. Guys, if you're married to a woman like this and she has a good-paying job or other types of income coming in, it will not help the situation at all. She will try to make you believe that she should not have to help take care of anything in the marriage. She wants you to believe that it is solely your job to take care of her.

The fact of the matter is that God created the woman to be a helpmate to the man; you are no longer two people but one in marriage. Your monies should be working together for the good of the whole, not for one person. A man who works hard, shows true love toward his wife, and provides a decent place for living is a good man. A woman who refuses to help her husband create the lifestyle set for both of them sees only herself in the marriage. This kind of woman is self-centered and does not fully understand what a marriage consists of. If you're a man struggling to pay the bills in a luxury lifestyle your wife desires to have, but she is not putting forth any effort to help maintain it; she's a sorry helpmate. For her to splurge on herself using her money to live a lavish lifestyle while her husband works overtime and, in some cases, two jobs just to please her desires; really, for real.

Guys, there isn't enough of any woman to be making a god out of, let alone bowing to her every demand. Wake up and smell the real roses. God said, "You shall have no other gods before me" and that means anyone or anything. No woman should ever be put on a pedestal because of her looks, how well she cooks, how good she is in bed, or how nice she treats you. If she's not working with you to maintain stability within the home or the lifestyle, then it's all about her. What I'm saying now is only about you and her, without children involved. If she's your girlfriend and you're doing all these things listed above; you're fooling yourself. It would be just a matter of time before the domino effect takes place, with her being the last domino standing; when she gets tired of all the things you're doing, all she has to do is raise her arm toward all the bills you have in your name, the debt you owe because of her, and what you have already given her. Once she pushes away from all the things you're doing just to please her, that's when the dominoes start to fall. Gust what? You will be the last domino to fall with the weight of everything on your shoulder.

Chapter 8

SAMPLING THE GOODS

I f you're still in the dating stage and you have not been contacted about the second date yet, now's the time to regroup. Instead of being anxious to see her the next time you meet, you should be thinking about gathering more information about her. As a veteran, I served during the Vietnam War. In training, we were taught many things about claymore mines as well as enemy mines. One of the key things I remember being taught was this: while in the jungle, keep your eyes constantly spanning your surroundings. If you step on something that sounds different than a dry forest leaf, stop in your tracks and don't move. Place a heavy object in the same place without moving your feet from the position you are in. That is, if you are traveling with other soldiers that can get you a big rock, strong enough to hold down the trigger button from igniting the fuse. Only then might you be saved from devastation.

For those of you who are new to the game of dating, listen up: This book will help you get through the forest of dating dangerous women. Don't play games with something that will blow up in your face. I've seen what land mines can do and I know what chlorobenzylidene malononitrile (tear gas) can do to your eyes and face. I compare all these things to a wicked woman who can and will destroy you if you let her. Use common sense, guys, use common sense in how you evaluate the situation. She may let you halfway sample the goods to get you stimulated to want more. Don't bite, guys; if she gives you one bite of one potato chip; she knows she's got you hooked. Try to see her in a more respectful and analyzing way when you're together with her. Allow your mind to actually see who she is and what she's all about.

However, her low-cut blouse allowing you to see half her basketballs and the short skirt or dress, a foot and half above the knees, should tell you to stop and think about what she's up to. Women who dress this way know exactly what they are doing. A woman who disrespects herself in this manner will have no respect for you. Trust me, I know what I'm talking about. This kind of woman may have come from a hard background and doesn't know what it means to respect herself. If you're a God-fearing man and want to keep God's commandments alive, don't think with your hormones in overdrive; know God's truth about the temptations of life. She is tempting you from many different angles of herself and you want to know what's really happening until it is too late.

A fish in the ocean sees a big juicy worm bobbing about and, without thinking, shoots over to grab it. In the fish's mind, it wants to grab the worm before another fish sees it. Little does it know that the worm had a hook in its body and, when the fish bit down on it, the hook stuck in its jar. That is when the fish begin to see its last days in the ocean, as it was being reeled in to become a good meal. Guys, don't end up in the frying pan of a woman who will have you for breakfast, lunch, and dinner.

The paragraph above was cut short so that what I said will stick in your brain. The temptation of a woman is one of the leading causes of men ending up in prison, falling through the cracks from being so naïve, unhappy because their back is against the wall with debt, fearful of losing their driver's license due to child support, and becoming a slave under her spell. The woman who lacks respect for herself has no foundation of truth. This in turn will create the lack of faith she has in a good man and cause herself to see him as a tool to get her needs met. A man who has his foundation built on truth, faith in God, and the will to do right can overcome these obstacles. A good man will take his time in getting to know a woman, to see if she is who she's pretending to be. A good man will not pressure a woman to open her legs just for his satisfaction. I know it is hard even for good men to hold back their own desires after having such temptation thrown at them. I say to you, my friends, be of good cheer, God has the right plan and the right woman for you. The only thing you need to do is be patient and look in the right places.

The question you might ask is: What do you mean by the right places? Think about it, guys: How often do men find virtually good faithful women in a tavern, at a wild and sleazy party, or in a whorehouse full of desperate women? These are not the kind of places I would say a good man should be looking for the right woman. The culture of people you associate with will cause you to become just like them. The world in which we live is full of temptations. Regardless of how hard we try to overcome our own weaknesses, our fleshly desire still lingers. That is why we need a foundation of truth and that truth is through Jesus Christ our Lord and Savior. If we walk by faith in Him, we can conquer all things while at the same time we are strengthened with His power to overcome our weakness. We do have the greater power within us if we believe in ourselves and in Him.

The power of knowledge and knowing the truth about these kinds of women will free you from a life of misery. If you walk by the sight of what you see: a beautiful woman, with a short dress a mile above the knees, and low-cut blouse with overflowing flesh bubbling out, you will fall into a pit. However, when you decide not to give in to the lustful thoughts of what you see but focus on your strength instead of your weakness, you will overcome. Your strength and determination come from the will and the love of God you should have in your life. Therefore, you will find yourself walking by faith, not by sight. We are in this world and not of this world. The people who are of this world will indulge in anything and everything this world has to offer. To be free from the pains and sorrows of life, you must become a new creature believing in Christ Jesus.

Life is a precious gift from God, although we fail Him because of the sins of Adam and Eve; He's giving us another chance through His son Jesus. Guys, if you don't get it right in the life that has been given to you, there will not be a second chance when you're done on planet earth. We should want to give our best and be our best at whatever we want to accomplish in life. Being with the right woman plays a big role in your success in life. True love is not based on how much money you have or how many tangible things you own, such as land, houses, gold, silver, or businesses. All of these things will be left behind after you disappear from the planet. Every breath you take is a blessing and an opportunity to enjoy the freedom you have to choose your direction in life. Don't waste your life with the temptations thrown at you from the Women of This World.

Chapter 9

KEEP HIM COMING BACK
FOR MORE OF THE SAME

An alcoholic and a drug addict have the same desires in common: to do anything necessary to get back to that feel-good state of mind. A devious woman will do the same thing to you if you let her. You will become addicted to her sexual luring, causing you to want her with a desire that makes your body ache for more of the same. Even when your eyes become open to the truth of what is really happening to you; you will ignore it, because it gives you the pleasure that makes you feel good. That, my friend, is what causes you to jump through hoops and over hurdles to please her for you to get what you want. You will not complain when she gets upset because you didn't have enough money to put down on her new Mercedes-Benz. Instead, you will get a second job or work more overtime. This is what the sex addiction will do to you; you will lose yourself in her desires.

If you're a single man dealing with issues like this, now's the time to get out and make your peace with God. If you're married, marriage is not a one-way street; it takes two to tango and two to make babies. If that be the case; you both should be walking toward the same goals in life, the ones that will benefit not just one but both of you. If you have married one of these devious women and have come into the truth of what she's been doing to him, there's still a way you can make it right. Sit down with her to discuss your marriage vows. Help her to understand her role as a wife and how you both should work together to make each other happy. If, after so many years of letting this go on, you find yourself afraid to speak up, then agree to see a good professional Christian counselor to make it right.

A pilot flying a plane at 60,000 feet suddenly has engine problems. The procedure he was taught to fix it is not working. He's now concerned for the safety of the passengers and wonders how he will land the plane without crashing. Out of desperation, he calls the airline's best mechanic to get instruction on how to correct the matter. After nearly an hour of conversation with the mechanic, he begins to follow the instructions given him. After several minutes of corrective procedures, the engine is finally back online and working as it should have. Guys, if your woman is having engine problems (anger, bad attitude, arguing, and never satisfied), it's time to call the best mechanic (Christian counselor) you can find. There's always hope, even in the worst of times; don't let your fear cause you to crash and burn.

Good airlines keep passengers coming back to use their services because they know how to keep their planes running safely and flying smoothly. Isn't that's the way a marriage should work when a good man takes full control of the cockpit (the problems) in the relationship? It's no wonder that marriages and relationships fall between the cracks. There's no platform to stand on, no real pilot flying the plane, and no foundation of truth to build on. Guys, if you want stability in flying the plane as it should be flown; take control in the right way. Don't be led by a self-centered woman who controls you by feeding you the same dog food every other night. You may have got used to eating it but, if you make up your mind and take full control; you'll enjoy better food and the amenities that come with it.

Check this out, guys: Adam was standing next to Eve in the Garden of Eden when satan told her it was okay to eat of the forbidden fruit that God said they should not touch. Because of her stubborn behavior, she stepped out of line from being Adam's helpmate to taking full control of making decisions for them both. She took from the tree in the center of the garden growing the forbidden fruit and did eat then turned around and gave to her husband Adam to do the same. Instead of Adam being the man that God gave control to he, became the follower to the woman. It is because of his dumb, dumb behavior and not following God's plan of instructions that we, as his descendants, are suffering that same faith today. If Adam had stepped up to be the man that God called him to be, he would not have been kicked out of the garden.

The only thing we have now to keep us in line with knowing who we are and our role as part of humanity is the word of truth from God Himself. This is the foundation we need to build on to live a better life with the opposite sex. "For God so loved the world that he gave His only begotten Son." The message that Jesus gave us is eternal life to those who are willing to follow His commandments to life here on earth and the hereafter. A person should prove himself to be worthy of the role that has been given to him in life. Guys, if you're not going to step up to the plate to be a real man and lead with love, righteousness, and honesty, then you are truly staying in the loop with Adam.

A young man named Esau sold his birthright for a bowl of soup. This young man had every opportunity to make his own meal. However, after being in the field all day, he found himself too tired to do anything to feed himself, so he went over to his brother Jacob and said, "Give me some of your soup." His brother Jacob replied, "Only if you give me your birthright." Throughout human history, men have done some crazy things to get what they want in life. I tell you of a truth, guys, a devious woman will con your soul from you if you let her. Many of you are like Esau, you want what can fill your empty desires now or make you feel good now. You're willing to give her whatever she wants in exchange; sounds familiar.

Esau is still trying to get back his birthright to this very day; look at what is happening in the Middle East. The woman who took your manhood and everything you gave up has left you high and dry. When you had a chance to get out, you didn't, you stayed because she gave you a feel-good reason. Now you are stuck with debt that you may never find freedom from, regardless of how hard you try. For some, starting over may only fill the empty hole with the trash they still have hanging on their shoulders. Going back for more of the same could cause rapid aging, loss of freedom, blind abuse, and a financial crisis. Stop, look, and listen to what I am trying to get you to understand. You are only going to pass this way once in your life. Why not make the best of it by giving yourself to someone, who will truly appreciate you, for who you are, and for the good that is within you.

Chapter 10

GIVING HER BEST SHOWING WHILE STILL FRESH

Prostitutes who stand on the street corner are honest women, in my opinion. They display their profession by how they dress and the way they try to get your attention. They want men to know who they are, by going to the extreme in showing the goods upfront and allowing you to see what you're getting and paying for. As nasty as this profession may be, the men who gravitate toward this type of behavior do have control over how much they are willing to spend for a few hours. Very seldom do you hear of a man finding himself in deep debt over a prostitute. There's a day-and-night difference between a prostitute and a con-woman. A prostitute is honest about who she is; a con-woman is deceptive and devious in many ways. It may be a long time before you truly understand what a con-woman is up to. When your thinking light finally clicks on, it may or, in some cases, may not be too late to end it or get out.

A man was invited by his friend to come by and watch the ball game on his big-screen TV. Upon entering his friend's house, he saw a bowl of juicy red delicious apples and could not resist asking for one. His friend said, "Help yourself, that's what they're there for." He grabbed one that looked the juiciest and took a big bite of it. As he was chewing, he noticed that something tasted meaty. Not wanting to embarrass the host, instead of spitting it out, he quickly finished chewing and swallowed. After swallowing what was in his mouth, he looked at the apple, turned it around, and saw a brown spot with a pencil hole leading into the apple core. The man had failed to examine the apple front and back before proceeding to eat it. The entire worm was swallowed in the first bite he took; which gave him plenty of protein during his first chewing.

The damage was already done; instead of the man swallowing his pride and spitting the chewed apple out from his mouth, he instead swallowed the chewed portions to save face. Guys, a woman might come on to you looking juicy and fresh, someone that could have no wrong in them. I tell you a truth: no one is without sin; she may look fresh and juicy on the outside but she could be loaded with problems for you on the inside. If you're one of those good men looking for an honest woman to pair up with; make sure you check thoroughly about who she claims to be and what her past has been like. However, if that's not important to you and you feel it's too time-consuming, then go for a woman you know is being honest upfront. With a prostitute, at least you know upfront what she is and why she enjoys what she does. Guys, realistically, that is not what this book is about; I am trying to open your eyes to the truth of what lies ahead in these kinds of situations.

Anyone can dress up and look like a professional; they could even talk like one. But I think we know all too well that is not always the case. The biggest cases we all see right now in this year 2021 are happening in Washington, DC. Politicians who claim to be for the people but in essence are there to satisfy themselves. This is why the kind of women in Washington, DC, can show their devious and conning behavior; it is because people like her put her there. Any woman can fool the masses of people about how good she can be for them, then, after settling in, turns out to be a self-centered moron. How much less or more do you think a single woman with this type of behavior will do to you as one guy?

Knowledge is power; it can be used to do good or bad. Many women in different levels of professions are no different than the women who have ulterior motives of taking advantage of a man. The only thing that can save you from the backlashes of an evil woman, whether in a personal relationship or one that's in politics, is the truth; it is the truth that will set you free. However, there isn't a whole lot that can be done for those who want to believe and live a lie. It may be because they themselves have exterior motives and want to allow such things to take place. Well, whichever may be the case, my goal is to help those of you who want to be honest with yourselves and find a virtuous good woman to partner with. Only then can you find the freedom and happiness that is meant to be in a good and fair relationship.

Chapter 11

PREPARING FOR A HOPEFUL LOCKDOWN

I f you are still single and have broken through the iceberg of trying to get to know the woman you've been dating for the past month, stay alert for strange behaviors; that is, if you haven't already noticed. The goal of a sweep-you-off-your-feet woman is to prepare you and put you in a lockdown state of mind in wanting to settle down with her. Don't let yourself become overwhelmed with her lustful looks, low-cut blouse, short skirt, and Jezebel makeup face. She's the kind of woman who can be compared to a black widow spider, a woman that makes a venom that affects your nervous system. Some men are slightly affected by it but others may have a severe response to her bite. Some may feel the attack right away or may feel severe pain, burning, swelling, and redness at the site where you've been bitten. You may even see two fang marks after breaking loose from her bite. So many good men start out on the good foot but in many cases end up in survival mode after the effects of the venom.

A half-dead man is no good to a good woman who is looking for Mr. Right. A good woman who is looking for a man who will treat her right by providing and taking care of her will be very disappointed hearing about your handicapped situation. "Handicapped" means that you are now bankrupt and in debt up to your ears from your last relationship. My friends, it does not have to be this way. The black widow spider woman will suck you dry and leave you for dead. If you can't get your life back in order after such a tragedy, it would be wrong for you to be looking for a good woman to take care of you. You would then become no different than the monster who took you down. I say monster because you would have allowed her to overpower you with her femininity, bringing you down similar to what Delilah did to Samson.

Throughout history, women have shown the ability to overpower men in many different ways; they are cleverer and smarter today than ever. I've been a professional psychology counselor for many years and I spent years obtaining an education that would accelerate me to higher levels in life. When I talk to many of the men and women who are struggling in bad relationships, I have found that many of the women are using psychology in ways that just blow me away. Most of these women have never studied psychology but they use it unconsciously and are very successful at getting what they want from men. Many of these women have come from generations of women who have practiced this behavior for years and have passed it down to their daughters. Each generation gets better and better at the tricks of the trade in what they do to get their needs met.

One of the ways a woman of this nature will try to get the man to marry her is by getting close to his male friends. She may act flirtatious through her conduct and the way she looks at them. She's making several plays by doing this: watching his reaction toward his friends and hoping his friends will later give him feedback about how attractive she is. Her goal is to get his friends to encourage him to marry her. By letting him see the good close relationships she's having with his friends, she sends him a message that he should get hooked up now or lose her to another fisherman. I have mentioned many times in this book the downfalls of thinking with your hormones along with the lustful thoughts in your head. They will cause you to make bad decisions just when you think you have everything under control.

Intelligent thinking will help override the pressured ideas that may cause you to make a rushed decision. You will begin to see the real woman behind the attractive looks and smile. Your eyes will open to the different moves she makes around your friends and her conning and flirtatious behavior shown in front of you. Your friends might enjoy it, but imagine this same type of behavior after you marry a woman like this. Can you expect her to truly be faithful to you as the years go by? A good man who pays attention to details should not have to fall into a mousetrap. However, many of them do because they fail to see through the dark (this evil woman) clouds that surround them. A foundation built with true love and respect will last for many years. One that is built with lies and deception will create great pain and hardship through the years.

However long it takes for her to understand your strengths and weaknesses, rest for sure that she will know how to use that information in a very smart way. Earlier in this chapter, I shared with you the psychology women use to seduce men. She may look like Mrs. Goody-Two-Shoes who can do no wrong; however, small packages have big surprises inside just waiting to blow up in your face. Every human being on the planet has weaknesses, some have more than others. It is our weaknesses that create our downfalls in life. How do we counter that? By taking off the old man and putting on the new man. You may ask, How do we do that? There are a number of ways; start by looking at how you operate as a man, the way you think, how you see yourself, how you see women, and, most of all, the foundation that you build your life on. You will never be able to do it alone; you need the foundation of truth, love, and righteousness. The only way to achieve this is by having Christ Jesus as the guiding light in all that you do in life.

When a man asks a woman for her hand in marriage, it should not be out of lust for her body, the way she looks, or how much money she has. It should be out of pure love and true affection with a desire to work through any problems that may occur. You, being the man, should show positive leadership with a strong desire to be fair when decisions are being made, taking time to hear her opinions on major issues that affect the lifestyle within the marriage. A good man should be leading his family, not following them. Most women expect a man to protect them from all hurt harm and danger and from the violent behavior of others. You are the strong holder in the house; if a thief breaks in you should protect her with your life. Guys, don't be a "Samson" to any woman; you will fall on your face every time. The woman was created to be your helpmate, not your controller or goddess to be worshiped. Take back the rightful place that God has given you, lead and be in control, be the head and not the tail.

It's not at all surprising that so many women are in full control of the household. Too many of you guys have become a "Samson" and are being pulled by the ring in your nose. The Creator of all life, the heavens, and the earth showed us what it takes to maintain respect and good leadership within His Kingdom. There was war in heaven at one time; satan (as beautiful as he was), was the head angel. He was God's trusted angel to do the things God had commanded him to do. After a long period of heavenly time had passed, satan decided he was no longer going to bow down to God. He felt that he was as powerful as God. and yet it was God who created him. One-third of the heavenly host of angels followed satan's lies about God. The short end of the story is this: God kicked satan and his followers out of His Kingdom to eternal damnation. They will never ever have the freedom that was given to them at their creation. God made it clear for all to see: He is not the tail but is the Creator of all things. He created man in the likeness of His image and the woman from the man to be his helpmate. Guys, God Himself is saying to you: Be what I have created you to be, the head and not the tail.

This same devious, deceptive, and con artist angel "satan" who tried to overrule God in His kingdom is now using many weak-minded women to follow him. When you don't understand who you really are, it opens the door for satan to enter in and encourage you to do his bidding. The generational sin and curse of a devious con-woman can be broken with knowledge and understanding of her true role in life. However, one must have the heart to want to change; satan is the father of lies and deception and it is he who will keep the blinders over her eyes. A good man will be led by the spirit of God in looking for a good woman to marry. He will see her deceptive moves, hear her lying words, and see behind all the makeup on her face.

Guys, when you decide to marry a woman; it should not be based on someone else's opinion or what they think of her. If you have done your homework by getting to know her, her family, and her past relationships over a good period, you then have the answers you need. Keep in mind that this should not take place overnight. If you truly like a certain woman and are considering spending a great deal of time with her, invest the weeks and months in getting to know for yourself how you feel about her. A lifetime commitment is about how you feel and not about what your friends or close family members think of what is best for you.

A deceptive woman can fool friends, family members, and close associates into thinking that she's the right woman for you. Family and friends may have good intentions of wanting to see you with the right woman; however, they will not be there to see what goes on behind the closed doors after the dust has settled. That is why you should educate yourself about who you're getting involved with before hearing what everyone else has to say. The final decision should be based on what you truly know to be the right answer for you. Why? Because of the time you've invested in her to obtain the answers, you need to make your own personal decision.

Chapter 12

SETTLING DOWN TO A NEW LIFE

After settling down with a con-woman, things may go well for a good little while. What she is doing, in essence, is building up your confidence in her as a good wife with a long rope tied around your neck. As time goes by, her practice of getting you under her control takes place slowly, giving you plenty of loving however you want it, while at the same time requesting small favors or tangible things to satisfy her desires. This behavior does not always take place overnight; months could go by before it starts. Each time she whispers in your ear during a loving time, she's pulling the rope of control around your neck closer and closer to herself. Now listen up, guys, when that rope is close enough for her to reach out and put her hands directly on you, you're in trouble. After a period when she can't get what she wants from you, be sure of this: you won't be getting your rocks off that night, I don't care how horny you are.

Your reaction may start out subtly or passively and yet inside you are very angry. You know you won't be getting much sleep that night because your hormones won't back down. Now she has you in the position of making you dance to her music using sex. She has spoiled you with sexual satisfaction in ways you can't describe. Then suddenly it stops over a request that you refuse to carry out. She may refuse to give you the benevolences you deserve as a husband for a few days or until you cave in to her selfish desires. Guys, once this process starts and you do surrender to her wants, you will become her slave and not realize it's happening. Why? Because you can't stop thinking about how good she satisfies you in bed. You might say, "Well, what's wrong with that?" If you know the request being made is going to (1) put you in debt beyond what you can afford to pay and (2) cause you to have to get a second job just to keep up with her demands, that's reason enough to see that she does not care about you.

A good man would sit his wife down to discuss the request she's making and how it could put them both in a financial crisis. However, if she refused to hear anything you have to say in the area of being reasonable, (concerning the problems it would cause) then you would know that it's all about satisfying her. If two people who are married become one before God and yet they cannot agree together, they are living in a divided house. Every man deals with issues like this differently; however, if you're married to a con-woman, the handling of the situation can be unpredictable in many ways. A con-woman will do whatever it takes to get what she wants from the man she feels she has control of. That is why so many good men end up becoming the tail toward the end of the relationship: They fail to see what is happening to them.

When their eyes are fully open to what is happening to them, it's too late for many good men, the damage is already done. He's drowning in debt, working two jobs, barely making ends meet, and then he decides to file for a divorce. In the process of waiting for a court hearing date, she moves everything out of the house while he's at work. She skips town with a U-Haul full of furniture he's still paying for, along with everything he owns. Then she has the nerve to ask her new boyfriend to drive her to another state. Now guys, if that doesn't make your balls drop down to the floor, I don't know what will. I am giving you the facts of things like this happening every day. I have counseled people who have gone through the very things I am sharing with you now.

Wake up, my good friends, a relationship does not have to be this way, nor does it have to end that way. Good morals and values do not come from beer taverns, bars, gang-banging, street corner women, or wild and sleazy parties. It comes from good training and good teaching about how to live a life that will be respectful to yourself and others. One must understand who he/she is and what they hope to achieve in life as a person. For that to take place, you must have a foundation of truth to build your life on, something to believe in that will help keep you on track with your goals in life. It's not enough to have faith in yourself because your body and mind become weak to the temptations of this world. You will find yourself lusting after things that make the body feel so good; you become prey every time you see it.

A person can overcome all of these obstacles by allowing Christ Jesus to become the center of his life. We all need a foundation of truth to stand on when making any kind of decision in life. Faith in yourself alone is not enough to achieve full success in this world. You will fall every time from leaning on your own understanding. Keep in mind you are made of flesh and blood, full of sin, and will never ever be perfect in this world. There is only one man that has ever walked the planet in perfect form without sin: God in the flesh of Jesus Christ. I tell you, my good friends, greater is He who lives within you than he that lives in this world; you will be able to conquer all things. The foundation of truth I am talking about is accepting Christ Jesus as your Lord and Savior. Put your trust in Him because He will never steer you wrong in whatever decision you are trying to make.

Guys, the best relationship you could have with anyone is with Jesus Christ; without Him, you don't exist. He is your Lord and Savior if you let Him take control. He will give you the right answers to all of your problems, save you from your own sinful nature, and make you equal heir with Him within the kingdom of God. Living by bread alone is not enough; you need the love and wisdom of God to guide you through the perils of life. Trying to find a good woman should be like trying to find yourself in all the good things you want to accomplish in life. Someone with similar desires to yourself would allow you both to walk in unity. However, in everything you do, you should be careful. Putting your trust in God, you will never be disappointed; putting your trust in man/woman, you will fall on your face and take a long time to recover.

Don't be that guy coming home after a hard day's work; you open the front door and find that she's taken everything, including the kitchen sink. Being a good man is not enough to live in this world. I don't care how good you think you are, evil will attack you in every area of life. The foundation of truth through Christ Jesus will help you find the right woman. Why? Because, when you put your trust and faith in Him, He will guide you to the right woman; she will have similar attributes to that of your own. When you meet a woman with a different outline to life and she doesn't have a foundation to prove it on, it would be like two people walking on different sides of the street, but heading in the same direction. Do you really think you could live with a person like that?

Chapter 13

DEALING WITH LIFE'S CHANGING TIMES

Regardless of where you are in life, change will continue to take place as you move up in age. Even in a good relationship, couples allow change to take place in order to keep the fire of love burning. I started driving a car at the age of sixteen and, throughout the years, I have never had any of my cars run out of gas. Each time I get into a vehicle, I check to see if I need to fuel up. Doc, what does that have to do with anything you're talking about here? It has everything to do with it: Think about what I just said, then look at relationships all over the world. To keep your marriage or boyfriend/girlfriend relationship alive, you must keep it filled with love, joy, peace, longsuffering, gentleness, goodness, faith in each other and in God, meekness, and temperance; without this, your car will run out of fuel really quick. You'll find yourself living under the law, in and out of courtrooms trying to solve problems that could have been avoided. When you maintain all of the attributes of love and the fruits that follow it; you will never be stranded on the side of the road.

Tom Hank, who played Forrest Gump said, "Life is like a box of chocolates; you never know what you gonna get." My response to that is this; yes, it can be true if you're lusting for a woman who has a certain body built and she's looking awesomely attractive. Men who don't research the ingredients that make up this kind of woman may not like what she tastes like. However, a man who's serious about his taste in women and is careful of who he's dating will do his homework first. He will take his time and not try to sample the goods before making a commitment. He will compare her value system to his, check out her beliefs in life, get to know her past and present situation, and, finally, decide if there's compatibility for a strong relationship.

If you chose the first option, you may find that some of the candy in the box has ingredients that could cause skin rashes, or you could be allergic to certain types of nuts or oils that may cause very bad health. Guys, I do hope you are reading between the lines of what I'm saying. I often write in metaphoric terms to help you see the logical point of view.

Dealing with change as you get older can and will take you out of your comfort zone. Young men who start out playing Monopoly (using women for their sexual satisfaction) will find out later in life, when they do get serious about settling down; their karma may come back to them in the same way they used women, by marrying a con-woman.

Guys, know this: What goes around comes around to you in many different ways. Don't think that, just because you decide to straighten up and fly right after five or ten years of abusing women just for sex, it is going to suddenly go away. No, no, no, my friends; the balance of life will not let you get away with such behavior. Even if you do find a good, kind, and loving woman who will treat you fairly, I can assure you that, somewhere down the road, you will face the consequences of how you treated the women who thought you were the right guy. Instead, you used them in the same way a con-woman uses a good man. If you're truly a good man and want to do right, don't let the temptations of any woman make a monster out of you. You will regret it with time, when you think it's all behind you and when you least expect it.

When I was a young man, I acted as a young man, ignorant of many things in life. In early 2000 I wrote a book called *Breaking Through Poverty with a Spiritual Heart*. In this book, I shared details about how young women would try to use me for their own purposes. I was very ignorant about the behavior of women then and found myself in trouble many times. The older I got, the more I learned from my experience of being around women, who were after me for different reasons. Many of the women who mistreated me later got involved with men who mistreated them in many different ways. Don't get me wrong, I'm not saying I was an angel of a young man; on the contrary, I was tempted by women in the same way some of you are being tempted today.

However, my foundation of truth was and still is to this day solid and very stable. My foundation is built on righteousness, truth, love, and fairness. Have I been stable in all these areas? No, I have not; I have fallen many times, got back up, knocked the dust off, and started over again to get it right. That is why I am writing this book to help you see yourself in the way you approach women and how women approach you. I am a retired, settled-down man doing the things God has gifted me to do. However, my ill-mannered behavior as a young man did come back to bite me. I saw this coming many times over the years, before and after retirement. This, my friend, is called the balance of life; what you did yesterday and today, be it good or bad, will come back to bite you tomorrow. For the most part, my life turned out to be very successful.

Young men, middle-aged men, and older men, don't let the sweet-smelling perfume and the soft lips with sounds that have warm air flowing through your ears, as she whispers sweet nothing, causing you to fall asleep at the steering wheel. Some may never wake up, others may wake up from a big crash with twisted metals around their body, unable to move due to broken bones. Some will end up in a trauma unit or a mental institution due to PTSD, and the ones who are permanently disabled will end up in a wheelchair for life. Guys, to understand what you're reading, you need to have a good level of comprehension of what you're reading. What you've just read is about a con-woman destroying the very person that you are today and she will take away your happiness and joy tomorrow. All of this will be determined by how deep you fall into her devious and cunning desires, just to satisfy her hunger for tangible things and much more.

All of us, from the time we were infants, have gone through growing pains to get to where we are today.

Growing pain and change coincide to make the changes needed to get through life. Growing babies fall countless times learning how to walk before finally getting it right. I am sure all of you understand the process of growth from a baby, to a child, to an adolescent, to a teenager, and finally to an adult. If you had good parents who taught you well during all four stages of growth, you should understand the process of decision-making as an early adult.

However, in today's world, that isn't so easy; with so many options to choose from, activities to get involved in, and temptation all around to throw yourself into, it's no wonder that so many good men fall on their faces half the time. Humans are not the only things that are changing; the world and all that is within it are constantly changing. Change is unpreventable and no one can stop it from progressing. The good things that take place and the bad things that take place will continue. But you as an individual must choose between the good and the bad. For some, that can be hard to do because they have no real foundation of truth to stand on. They have no real moral compass or values to live by; it's more like, whichever way the wind blows, I'll go in that direction.

We are all created with a special DNA that separates us from the billions of people around the world. This DNA makes us truly unique in every way. Therefore, we must search from within ourselves to find what it is we truly want in life and not follow through on what everyone else is doing. When a person follows the crowd without analyzing the facts of how it will affect them, they tend to give up their rights allow themselves to be led by others. It's easy for many people to sit in the back seat of a car and let someone else do the driving without knowing where they're going. Then, when you get there, you're not happy with what you see and wish you had taken control of your own driving to get yourself to a better location in life.

Most men who don't put enough thought into their lives end up this way. Birds flying through the air tend to show more concern for their safety and the locations to where they land for food and rest than most people. They are very careful of what is in the area and who is in the area before landing on anything solid. Guys, an unstable woman is unstable in all her ways and will rock your boat to sinkable levels. That is, if you're not careful in familiarizing yourself with the landing zones.

Chapter 14

THE CLOAKING CHANGES
IN HER BEHAVIOR

Many women who start out as good women, with intentions of being good supportive wives to their husbands, end up becoming con-women. You might ask: "How is this possible?" Easy, most women love to hang together with other women and some like being in different groups. Women, like some men, do enjoy sharing the behind-the-scenes of what goes on at home. Guys, I have to tell ya, as time passes in the relationship, whether it be months or even years; you will start to see changes in behaviors. The culture of women she may be involved with may have poised her mind to believe she can get more from you if she intensifies her attitude and behavior. In other words, being more demanding of the things she wants, that she knows you can't afford but wanting you to get it anyway. She does this by holding back your evening love snacks, your bedtime dessert, and giving you the cold-shoulder goodnight.

After months or years of marriage, you have seen many disagreements in the past and may see this as just another glitch in the relationship. You may shake it off, thinking she's on her monthly cycle. Things do get better later but then the subject pops up again on a different day and time.

Guys, she's cloaking her way into training you to dance to her music. However, you've become too naïve to see the changes that are coming your way. Her friends are starting to control how she should treat you in a subtle way but, as time passes, it gets more intense from her end. When you finally cave in to getting her what she wants and you're now working plenty of overtime to get it paid for, you're happy, thinking that will be the end of it. But little do you know that was just an appetizer for the big things to come. Keep in mind she's not working and is totally dependent on you for whatever she needs and wants.

There is nothing wrong with a woman just wanting to be a housewife. However, if you, the husband, have a good-paying job and you are living within your means of income, why go beyond what you can't afford? If you do, and your wife is capable of working, she should want to help take some of the financial burden off you. If the financial budget you both currently have is giving you a good lifestyle, going beyond it should mean working together to raise the standards. If suddenly she wants things that will take you out of your comfort zone but she is not willing to help alleviate some of the financial pressure, she's now turning into a con-woman. A woman who has stopped appreciating her husband's effort to make life comfortable is now using him to satisfy her own selfish greed.

A good relationship depends a great deal on the culture of people you associate yourself with. We all have different lifestyles, different beliefs, different behaviors, different attitudes, and different views of how we see ourselves in the world. If your foundation is built on lies and deception, you will sink and drown over a short or long period. Leaning on your own understanding about life and living in this world is not enough; you need a higher power of control. The faith you both may have in each other may get you to where you think you're comfortable in the life you're living; however, it will be just a matter of time before the house of cards comes tumbling down. Rich man or poor man, each will find the foundations of this world will never stand up to the hard winds and the heavy rains that fall in our lives at times. There is only one true foundation to live on, the foundation of righteousness through Christ Jesus, Who died to save us. One day heaven and earth will pass away but God's righteousness will live on forever.

Guys, this is the greater power I was telling you about earlier. When you tap into this power, all things are possible through Him that is within you. You will no longer want to hang out with people who don't think the way you and your wife do. When you see that their foundation is not as stable as yours, you will want to break ties with them because you know it will infect your marriage. When you associate yourself with people who undermine each other with lies and confusion about life and marriage, you become just like them. After a while, you will find yourself losing the respect you once had for each other. Life is too short to be listening to the antics of other people's ideas about life, especially when you know that their foundation is only filled with lies and the deception it will cause if you practice it.

If you're a man of integrity and want to do right toward your wife and you want your wife to do right toward you, then stop and look at what you both have accomplished together over the years. If you both built all that you have through love and being faithful together and you do have a solid foundation of truth through Christ Jesus, what more do you need to keep you on track? When you have this greater power to help you in the sanctity of your marriage, and you understand the process of how to use it, don't let others try to fix something that is not broken. Stand with your faith unwavering in God because the world will try to destroy you if you let it. A good wife does not have to go "con" due to friends with bad behaviors. If she has a good husband who knows how to lead, he should be able to help her stay on track. However, a husband that does not know God's truth will fall by the wayside like the seeds from a garden pot. At which time the birds, squirrels, and other seed-eaters will come and devour him and his wife before they can understand what is happening.

Chapter 15

UNAPPRECIATIVE AND UNSUPPORTIVE

Relationships can be unpredictable when getting to know each other. A deceptive con-woman will in most cases be on her best behavior, especially when she finds a really good man who's willing to work hard to make her happy. Con-women are not all the same in how they operate. Some will not do research on a man to find out who he really is and what he's all about. Many will base it on his behavior that takes place in front of them; how he conducts himself, his conversation, his appearance, and so on. However, others may take precautions and do a full background check to make sure they come out of the relationship in one piece. A woman of this nature has already planned out what she's going to do with the man and how she plans to use him. She's being smart to avoid finding a man who will kill her for her dirty deeds toward him.

The man who fails to do what the woman is doing to protect herself may suffer a great hardship toward the end of the relationship. Regardless of how smooth of an operator she is, the livelihood of your joy and happiness depends on what you do to protect yourself. It may not be easy trying to obtain information about a woman; however, when all else fails to give you what you need, put your faith in

God to give you the answers you need to move forward. If, after a period of time, you decide to lock hands with this woman; you still need to keep your eyes open to how well she acclimates to the new lifestyle. A woman who is truly happy is a woman who loves you for who you are and not just what you can do for her. The signs will begin to show where she really stands as the months and years pass you by. A good woman will appreciate the little things you do and show you with plenty of hugs and kisses. On the other hand, a con-woman may thank you and give you a fake smile. As time goes by, the good woman is happy and content with what you are doing to make you both happy. She does not complain because she knows the financial situation can only do so much for their lifestyle.

The con-woman over a period of time will not look at the big picture of what is going on in the household. Instead, she will start longing for things that go beyond their financial budget. She may show signs of not being happy with the way things are currently going. This could be the beginning of signs revealing that she never really loved you for the man that you really are, but for only what she could get out of you. A good woman who desires things outside the budget will offer to get a job to help in supporting the overflow of bills. The con-woman will tell you what she wants, then suggest you get a second job or work overtime to get it paid for. Because of her lifestyle with her girlfriends, she will not make any efforts to get a job to help in paying any of the overflow bills. When you see this type of behavior starting to take place, you need to reexamine the relationship and discuss the reasons for the sudden change. It is one thing to be unappreciative in the relationship but is a major problem when you are not being supported in what you're doing. Relationships should be built on supporting one another's efforts to make it work, whether in a marriage or a long-term dating stage.

Men will not find these attributes in a con-woman due to self-centeredness. When I was a kid growing up, I had to walk through a wooded trail that had many trees and small forest growth. The area had many poisonous snakes and small wild animals hidden inside. As soon as I hit the trail my eyes would scan every step before I took it. I wanted to make sure I did not run into snakes laying across the path or a small wild animal that could bite me. After a while and seeing other kids walk the same trail, I became more comfortable and begin to drop my guard. One day when I got up late and was running late for school, I took off down the trail and was not scanning the area in the usual way. I nearly stepped on a large rattlesnake curled up in the middle of the path. I came within one foot of it and my heart nearly stopped beating; I backed up quickly, the snake uncurled and crawled back into the wooded area. From that day forward, I never dropped my guard and always scanned the area as I walked through those woods. I could have easily been bitten by that snake and probably would have died from the poison. Snakes can blend in well with their surroundings so that you cannot see them until you are right on top of it.

A con-woman is no different than a snake; she can come

at you in many different ways and tear you apart in another way. Her strike can make you sick to your stomach; and cause you to have ulcers, high blood pressure, and other types of sickness. People who play with live snakes expect to get bitten over time; it is what they like to do and they understand the risk they're taking. However, to avoid running into a con snake woman, you must continue to scan the relationship trail to make sure you don't get bitten.

Chapter 16

PARADING A GOOD SHOW OF HAPPINESS AMONG FRIENDS

Most relationships are very secretive behind the scenes; friends and relatives very seldom know the truth of what is really going on. A conwoman knows how to put on a good show among friends and relatives, just to keep their suspicious thoughts at bay. She will pretend she is so in love with the man she's with by holding on to his arm or kissing up to him in front of family and friends. This behavior could take place shortly after a big argument just before they left the house to visit others. In other cases, she may have guests over for dinner or they could be just stopping by to visit. In all these instances, she will put on a good show to keep the truth hidden. Good men go through abusive relationships as much as good women do. People very seldom hear about men being abused by their girlfriends or wives. Much of this has a lot to do with men not wanting to be put in the spotlight, showing them to be weak-minded and not in full control. A man does not want to be seen as a pushover boyfriend or husband around people they know. However, many of them will sacrifice being abused to keep an attractive woman who makes them look good around their friends.

The man may be on the verge of bankruptcy because she

has got him into so much debt, yet he continues to smile, thinking he's got a good thing. She may see him as nothing more than a railway to luxury stores, malls, and fancy travel to other countries. Many of these men think that they may never find another woman to accept them for who they are or give them the true love and support they deserve, so they tolerate a con-woman who has accepted them but shows very little love and hardly any support. What you become is a puppet held up on thin strings, enough to keep each part of you moving in one direction: the direction of satisfying her needs when and wherever she wants them met. Some good men don't mind becoming a slave to this kind of woman simply because they can't get enough of her ABC and all the side dishes that surround it.

However, there is another side to men who want to do their best to make the relationship work. Some will work hard trying to get the woman into counseling concerning her behavior within the relationship. Most men want to make their marriage work when finding out the kind of woman she really is. If she is cheating on him with someone else and it is discovered, this would give him a reason to part ways from her. But if her addiction to spending money and being married to herself is the biggest problem, there may be the hope of helping her see the light. Of course, divorces should only take place when one is cheating on the other or one person is being terribly abused by the other, physically, mentally, and/or verbally. No one should have to go through such pain in any marriage or dating relationship, unless they choose to do so and know the consequences.

Anyone can show signs of being happy in a bad situation from behind closed doors. However, the person who will suffer the most is the one who is tolerating the abuse and is doing nothing about it. If you are the one on the tail end of this whirlwind, after the dust settles, it may take you a long time to start over with someone new. Most good women shy away from a has-been man who is now carrying large debt and is barely able to take care of himself. I cannot say you won't be able to find one; the one you may find may be in the same situation as yourself. Trying to get two old and rundown broken cars to run will take a lot of hard work. It may be that you will have to take parts from one of the cars and put them into the other one to get it running. This process could take a very long time and could become very expensive in getting things to work. Don't let the two old broken cars become you; starting all over again.

Chapter 17

THREATENING TO WIPE
HIM OUT IF HE LEAVES

Women with devious behaviors can become very bold over a period of time. Men who have low-key ways of communicating, along with their calm demeanor when arguing with their mate, create the boldness in a woman to think she has more control. It gives rise to her wanting to yell more because she thinks you're too weak-minded to get your point across. If this is the kind of behavior that has been going on for long periods and she has managed to always get what she wants, then you as the man are giving her that power. She may think you have concerns about her leaving you if you don't bow down to her desires. However, that is not always the case with some men. A man with a low-key temper can be the most dangerous man a woman could be with. Some of these men act this way because they know if they rise to the same level as the woman, she could be in great danger from a terrible beating. A man who is quiet and does not like to argue can be the best supporter a woman could ask for. However, when a devious con-woman is yelling at this kind of man, he is thinking of all kinds of ways he could tear her apart or even kill her.

This is the kind of man who can be very passive at certain

levels of anger. This passive behavior can build and build from a level of passive-aggressive behavior to an aggressive point, where he is not in control of himself when he does act out. This kind of man could be a loving and caring husband or boyfriend until he can take no more of the abusive behavior. This is why there are so many good men in prisons today, because of women who provoke them to that level of anger. Guys, if your foundation of living in this world is built on sinking sands, you must understand you will sink and suffocate. If you're depending on self-control to get you through a bad situation, forget it. I have said it once and I'll say it again: You need a higher power to help stabilize your mind. In those trying times, the devil will put all sorts of thoughts into your head; he will show you ways to shut her up and make you feel justified in doing it. After you've followed through in hearing satan's suggestions and there's no more yelling to be heard, when the dust finally settles, you may find yourself in a room looking at the four walls of a 5-by-8 prison cell.

If you want true freedom from the pains and sorrows of what life is throwing at you, try Jesus. I guarantee that you will never see life in the same way again. He is truly a game-changer in every aspect of what you do in life. When your back is against the wall and you're trying to figure out how to solve a problem that is out of your control, He will give you the answers you need. The thing you have to do is put your trust and faith in Him and acknowledge Him in all your ways. He loves you so much and will never ever steer you wrong. That is why He gave His life on the cross:

to save you from yourself and your sinful behavior. Your act of righteousness by taking revenge on someone who has crossed you the wrong way; is foolishness before God. The wisdom of this world is foolishness in God's sight, which is why you should put your faith and trust in Him.

A woman who has become a bully to her man knows that, if he ever tries to leave, she should do something drastic to stop him. She knows that, once you leave, the luxury lifestyle stops in its track. She will make threats about what she will do to you and she will also tell lies to the friends you both know. She will do this to get people to feel sorry for her and to support her in whatever she will try to do to you. You must understand, a woman of this nature is not in love with the man; she's in love with what the man can do for her. There's a day-and-night difference between the two. You can't make someone love you for who you are. If they chose only to focus on what you can do, then you're just a tool to get things done.

You may get rewarded with sex if you do what you're told. Notice I said sex, not love and affection, which is what you should be receiving in all that you do throughout the relationship. Men who allow themselves to go to the extremes of trying to receive true love and affection from this kind of woman create their own destructive end. I have seen rubber balloons put on air machines to be filled with air. At one time I saw the person filling the balloons forget to take one off the machine. The balloon got so big from stretching its rubber out, it could do nothing else but burse from so much pressure built up inside. Guys, don't be an over-pressured balloon, thinking you are in full control of your actions; you won't be able to control the burst effects.

Chapter 18

USING SPECIAL FRIENDS
FOR A SUPPORT BASE

The people who are the closest to her are the ones she feels would never betray her; they are her cornerstones. These are the people who would believe anything and everything she says about you. Remember the topic "Parading a Good Show'? The whole purpose of putting on a good show is to make others think that you both are so in love with each other. Although you know that is not the case, you allow yourself to play along anyway. You may find it embarrassing for friends to know just what is really happening behind closed doors, so you dance to the music.

Some of you guys may have been raised by parents who acted in the same manner but, because of what you saw growing up, you decided you want to be different, so you try very hard to show this woman that you really want to make the relationship work. But you continue to close your eyes to what you know is happening around you. Most people are very private about their personal affairs with their mates. However, a vindictive woman will tell everyone in town about what she doesn't like about you or what you did to her. If you really make her angry, she may tell her special friends a bunch of lies to further hurt you.

A woman who can control certain friends outside of her household can be referred to as the ALPHA female. This type of woman inadvertently uses psychology to control how other women think and see her within the group. When that group meets, she takes control and places herself as the alpha leader. She dares anyone to disagree with her during conversation and those that do disagree are afraid to speak out. If anyone does challenge her, she will belittle them and cause the rest of the group to turn against her. Before selecting this special group of friends, she analyzes those who are easily susceptible to her seductive control. She will then privately meet with them on different occasions, to mold them to her liking and get them to bow down to her as their smart leader friend.

In the same way, a person who is planning to murder someone or rob a bank makes plans of how they are going to carry it out before it happens; this is called premeditated planning. The woman who goes out of her way to set up cornerstone friends as a special support base has big plans of wanting to hurt you later on. If you're a married man living with a woman like this, now is the time to seek counseling to help get her on the right track. However, if you are living with her and you have no children, get out of the relationship. On the other hand, if you think you can help her see her evil ways and she is willing to change, I say again, seek the help of a good Christian counselor.

Many of the choices we make are based on our common sense about truth and facts. However, we don't all have the same sense of truth and facts. Some may have been raised to believe lies and to be deceptive toward other people. What a person may have been taught to believe, may take years to break away from before accepting the facts of what life has to offer. If you're involved with a woman who has this upside-down behavior and she is refusing to seek help; you should use your common sense and do what is right for you. I just hope your common sense is more respectable and is within the law of doing right.

There is nothing wrong with having a good friendship support base, as long as it respects within the group. However, the person who manipulates their friends to do their dirty bidding hurts not only the one they are trying to destroy but their friends' families as well. Guys, you may have friends for a short period who stop associating with you because of what has been said about you. It may be months or even years before your friends find out the real truth. This is the damage that one person can cause to the relationship of many people who were good friends at one time.

A woman like this has no boundaries to the damage she's willing to inflict just to hurt you or get back at you for not satisfying her desires. She could fool the very elect by making them think she is the nicest and most respectable woman they know. Clever and conniving women like this do not need a pat on the back for pretending to be what they never are. They are self-centered and reward themselves in just about everything they do.

Chapter 19

WEARING THE PANTS AND THE DRESS

A good man who uses good judgment when leading his wife, girlfriend, or family hopefully has a good foundation of truth to lead by. Most household members depend on the man of the house to protect them from unwanted danger. However, if the man is not leading well and has fallen by the wayside, he's a disappointment to his woman. It is expected that most women would take positive control to help the man get it right or help him get back on track.

A dominating woman will jump at the opportunity to take full control of everything. You may not get the positive help needed to get you back on track as head of the house. However, you will pay a heavy price for being the tail instead. I had five sisters growing up and not one time did I ever see them wear pants, whether it was in or away from the house we grew up in. They were raised to look like young ladies with feminine behavior. The dresses they wore and the behavior they displayed, around their boyfriend or husband, showed a level of dependence on them for support; and to take care of them. Some of them also took jobs to help their husbands when needed.

Today's society is showing that there are nearly as many women in control of the household as there are men. I'm talking about men still living at home with their wives or girlfriends. Some of these women are acting the part of the man while being the woman in charge of everything. Guys, if you start out on the right foot in a relationship that had positive potentials, don't turn that good woman into a monster by your lackadaisical attitude of not being the man in charge. Maintain being the man that God has created you to be, the head and not the tail. There are enough men in our society who have chosen to be the tail for other men instead of being the head of a wife or girlfriend. As sick as it may sound, that's the world in which we live. Life's temptations can lead us in many directions, but having a strong foundation will prevent many of the abominations from taking place in our lives. I can tell you a lot of things about the behavior of devious con-women. However, only you can decide which side of the track you want to be on; in any relationship.

I want to take this time to speak to all of the men reading this book who are in relationships with women. Good or bad, guys, you need to know that your performance as a husband or boyfriend will determine the kind of feedback you will receive from your mate. If you are serious about holding on to one woman, you need to make her feel that she is the only woman you want to be with. Women are the weaker vessels and they need a good man who is going to take the role of a leader in their lives.

History has shown what happens to women when the man dumps her for another piece of ABC. They end up having to find jobs to support themselves and, in many cases, they work harder for less pay. They are tired of the games that men are playing on them. Many of them have seen enough of what is happening to their friends and are changing their approach to men in many different ways. This is why I have spent so much time writing about the different groups of women in our society today: Women who will love you and give you the respect you deserve, women who will play the same adulterated games you play, women who will make a slave out of you without you knowing it, and women who will work in partnership with you for higher living standards. The list could go on with other types of behaviors toward men.

The thing that I am trying to get you to see is this: If your foundation is weak starting out, you will fall into one of the categories listed above. A man who wants to do right for his woman should have a vision of the life he wants to give her. Being a good man is not enough; your actions should show who you really are, with the desire to give her a life full of love, joy, and true happiness. What you cast out is what you should get back from her.

However, a con-woman will not care about how good you are or what you are doing to try to make her happy; she just wants you to keep doing what you do until you drop dead. A man with a solid foundation of faith, hope, and love in God through Christ Jesus will have the wisdom from above to help him see through all of her behaviors; long before it causes him to fall on his face. Too much focus in one area will cause you not to see the real problems in other areas. Men and women should never take each other for granted; you must hold each other up in faith, hope, love, and respect. Without these elements in a real marriage or relationship that's trying to go somewhere, there can be chaos and confusion later on.

Chapter 20

CLOSING WORDS AND THOUGHTS

I started out writing about the behavior of devious con-women toward good men and what they look for in order to take control. I hope the information I have shared with you throughout Section I will help you make the right decisions in building positive relationships. Women who are reading this section of the book, please keep in mind that I have written in "Section II" about the criminal mind of corrupt men toward good women. I don't just feed one side of the fence and I am not biased toward women in any way. In fact, I am more sympathetic toward women than men.

Why? Because women are the weaker vessels and they get taken advantage of more so than men. So, men, I want you to know that I have a whole lot more to say to the women concerning many of the terrible behaviors some of you have and the games you like to play on them. So, take it with a grain of salt, many of you are not being truthful with yourself nor to your partner. However, I just pray and hope that this book will help open your eyes to the real truth of who you are and what you are doing right now. Good or bad, the day will come when we all have to answer for our dirty deeds in this life and the life or death to come after.

Guys, for those of you that are trying to do right but are being tempted on every side, break away from the culture of negative friends who are pulling you down to their level of behavior. Men who have no real morals or values in their lives can and will destroy other lives. Stop and look at who you are and how you want to represent yourself in society, how you want others to see you, and in what way—as a conniving, devious, evil terror or as someone with good manners who is well thought of by others, and is a good boyfriend or husband to your woman. A good man with a good reputation goes a long way in society. You will still be remembered long after you have left planet earth. A good-natured person who sets positive examples in life causes others to want to follow in his or her footsteps. Your actions, good or bad, influence others to want to be like you. You should be careful of the seeds you plant in society; your children, your close friends, and the people who may be watching you will be affected.

Section II

THE CRIMINAL MIND
OF CORRUPT MEN

Chapter 1

YOUR AWARENESS IN PUBLIC PLACES

G ood day to all the ladies preparing to read Section II of this book. Before you begin, grab yourself a good cup of tea, coffee, or your favorite cold beverage, then lie back in a soft recliner chair to begin your reading. First of all, I want to take this time to thank you all for allowing me to enter your hearts and minds to share what I have to say about men. Some of you may already have some knowledge about the behavior of men, while others may be in for a rude awakening to what their eyes will be reading. Whatever type of reaction you may have, I do hope it will open your eyes to the reality of what some men are all about. Please fasten your seatbelt; we will be flying at an altitude of about 60,000 feet. You're allowed to take breaks only when the green overhead light is on. Please have a nice flight. I will be talking with you again when the plane lands on the last chapter of this book.

The writing in this section of the book is sharing information with women who hold great respect for themselves: Women who want men to be patient, respectful, and honest with them. The women I am referring to show a day-and-night difference from those discussed in Section I of this book. They are women who take pride in themselves when they are out in public places. They try to be careful

94

not to draw attention to themselves in a sexual way by the outfits they wear. Although the book is for all women to read, I am especially trying to help those who hold strong morals and values in building good relationships.

Public places have been the backyard for corrupt-minded men for many years. Good women, sleazy women, and respectable women; these men have no respect for persons or whom they will target. They will look at you and fantasize about all kinds of ways they could have you for breakfast, lunch, and dinner. Ladies, I don't mean at an eating table, I'm talking about his bedroom, back alley, the backseat of his car, or somewhere in the bushes where no one can see you. Many of the men with this mindset have many things going on with them. Some of them have sexual additions, others get their kicks out of torturing you to death, some like to see the fear on your face, while others plan out their attack in a very clever and smart way. It does not matter how well-dressed the man may look or how intelligent he may talk, he may be a wolf in sheep's clothing.

I've had men tell me they only go to the park to watch the women and girls run and play. They are especially looking at what you are wearing, if they can see anything above the thighs that leads to your crotch area or within your chest line; that, in and of itself, will create lustful thoughts. It does not take much to set some men off on a path of sexual fantasy. I lived in South Korea for many years and saw men on crowded buses and subways brush themselves continually against women and young girls. They would grab their behinds and press themselves tightly to their butts.

This behavior also takes place in America in crowded cities everywhere. In these situations, it doesn't matter what you're wearing; it's the close encounters with so many people around you. The bad thing about that is that good men who try to be respectful will find themselves being tempted to do the same thing in those situations. Crowded transportation makes it easy for predators to get off at certain stops and never be found for what they did to you.

Ladies, public places can be some of the nicest and safest places to be in. However, if you're a woman that is naïve and assumes everyone is respectable in that environment, you would be making a grave mistake. Corrupt-minded men have no boundaries to where they look and prey on women and girls of all ages. You should make it your business to be very aware of your surroundings and who is watching you. You may be standing by your car to put groceries in the back seat and, before you can pick up the bags, someone grabs you from behind. The predator who grabbed you may have been parked right next to you in a van. In other cases, you may be at a town square, sitting on a bench with your little six-year-old girl and, while you're talking on the phone, she's having fun playing with other kids. The minute you turn and look the other way from your daughter, someone has put her in a car and drove off. You might think that this only happens to other people and you're too smart for that.

Ladies, ladies, I don't care how smart you think you are or if you think you would never let anything like that happen to you. People from every walk of life have made that same mistake, from the very richest to the poorest. This pattern of behavior is called a comfort zone for those that are in a relaxed state of mind. Here is a good example: People who may have lived in a quiet neighborhood for many years without any crime taking place would feel safe. However, when they hear about Sally, who left her front door unlocked and was upstairs when the rapist came through the front door and raped her in her own bedroom; that would be a rude awakening to everyone living in the neighborhood. There are many men in our society today who can be very unpredictable much of the time. Ladies, don't let your comfort zone become a rude awakening for you.

The warm days of the year are the hunting season for many corrupt-minded men, and I don't mean game animals; I'm talking about women and young girls. Those men know that the beaches, parks, malls, and event centers will be crowded with the kind of women and girls they are looking for. The kind with the short skirts, booty-tight pants that show the buttocks, low-cut blouses that reveal the two bumpers inside; and, at the beach; the nearly buck-naked and G-string women walking around having fun. Like lions in the bush, these men are waiting for the right moment to strike. They are very patient and are willing to wait as long as it takes for them to get what they really want. Many of them will blend in with the crowd, showing themselves to be normal people having fun. They will present themselves as being clean-cut and very friendly with everyone.

However, all of this may be a front just to get close to get to know you. If you're at a dance club or bar, that's even worse because now there's the opportunity to buy you many alcoholic drinks. This kind of place would be an easy catch for men with this kind of behavior. Good women who allow themselves to go to these places are almost asking to be taken advantage of. These men will toy with you all night until they get you in the mindset of trusting them, and that is when they will make their move. Eight hours later, you find yourself waking up in his bedroom and not knowing where you are. I don't believe most women want to find themselves in that situation. However, a respectable woman with strong morals and values would not put herself in such danger. Those that do may have low self-esteem and welcome the attention from the men's lustful behavior. I believe women who put themselves in such danger are trying to find love in the wrong places.

The way women dress in public places has changed tremendously. The mindset of women in the early 1700s (and even before) through the early 1900s is a day-and-night difference from what women and girls are wearing today. The loss of respect for themselves in public places has skyrocketed to an all-time high. Women, you must understand, you are not shaped like men, nor do you feel like men; you are what men are attracted to. Your looks, your shape, how your body feels, the sound of your voice, the way you taste, how you smell, and how you arouse them when they look at you are the elements that drive some men crazy about women and girls. Crazy enough to take away your humanity by forcing you to satisfy them in whatever kind of way they desire to be pleased.

Nowadays, it doesn't matter what women and girls wear in public places, stalkers are waiting and watching your every move, to catch you in a vulnerable place and or position to snatch you up to become a sex slave in this country or other countries. One of the key reasons why so many women and young girls end up missing in action is because they never think about it happening to them. The King James Bible tells us in the book of Philippians chapter 4:6; *"Be careful for nothing; but in everything by prayer and supplication with thanksgiving; let your requests be made known unto God."* When you think you have everything under control by yourself, that is when all hell breaks loose. Ladies, you need a greater source of power to keep you safe from all hurt, harm, and danger. Only through Christ Jesus can you have this true peace of mind when dealing with the wilds of this world day and night.

When I was a small boy, I use to enjoy playing with a little girl named Linda. One day we were playing in the front yard of the church, we were running and she fell onto small rocks and tore the skin in several places just below her right knee. We went and sat on the front steps of the church; she cried aloud and I felt so sorry for her. I tried to console her but there was nothing I could do. Her mother heard her crying and came to investigate what was wrong. She saw the bleeding and the scarred area just below her knee. She went into the church and came back with a bottle of alcohol, gauze, pads, and tape to dress the wound.

When Linda saw the bottle of alcohol, she tried to get away from her mom; she knew that it would burn worse than the current pain she was feeling. Her mother calmed her down and explained that it would only sting a little bit and that it would stop the bleeding much quicker.

The mother proceeded to take care of the wounded area and when she was finished, Linda had gauze pads and tape wrapped around the lower part of her knee. The next day when I saw Linda, she was happy, smiling, and ready to start playing again. However, I noticed there was a difference in how she played with me; she showed more awareness toward the area where she had been injured. Weeks later, she was still being careful how she played with me. I believe the experience she had caused her to be very careful of how she was interacting with me through playing. Ladies, I shared that story with you to help you understand what it means to have someone to protect you when you don't know what to do.

As a child, Linda depended on her mother to make the right decisions in making things better for her situation. Linda not only was taught to believe in God but also God used her mother to show love, care, and protection when she needed it. It doesn't matter whether you are family, friend, neighbor, or a total stranger on the streets, we are all interconnected as a people. God can use any one of us to protect the other from the hurt, harm, and danger that lies in this world. This is what I meant when I said to you that you need a greater power to protect you as you go through life's ups and downs.

Chapter 2

THE CULTURE OF THE WORKPLACE

T he workplace is almost as dangerous for women as being in public places. Blue-collar and white-collar workplaces are safe havens for criminal-minded men. Some women who work alongside men in these areas find themselves feeling very uncomfortable much of the time. In the early 1990s, I worked as a "Certified Cultural Awareness Trainer" for the state of Washington. It was a two-week class taught in many different state offices in western Washington. At every office I trained at, some of the state employees found themselves either crying or very angry at what was happening to them in the workplace. Ninety-nine-point nine percent of the complaints were from women being harassed, meddled with, receiving unwanted hugs, touched in unwanted places, hearing sex jokes, seeing undesirable porn pictures hanging on the wall, and being stared at while doing their job.

At each location, every employee, all managers, and all supervisors had to take this training class; it was made mandatory by the state of Washington. The class revealed things happening in the workplace that were unacceptable according to state standards. Most of the corrupt behavior came from men who were in management or supervisory positions. The excuses many of them gave during the class discussion was, "I didn't know she felt that way," or "I was just being friendly," and the ones who liked putting their arms around women would say, "I was just showing my appreciation for your help." These and a mountain of other excuses were shared during these workshop sessions. There were a few men who showed remorse for what they did and a few wiped the tears from their eyes due to the embarrassment they faced.

When a woman finds herself the minority in the workplace, you can rest for sure that she will be targeted for sexual favors or harassment if she rejects their interest in her. Ladies, there's nothing wrong with looking nice and presentable in the workplace. However, when you come to work wearing short skirts, up to your bloomers, and low-cut blouses that reveal your beach balls, you are asking for attention. This attention, in most cases, will not be the respectful attention you think you will be getting. What you will be doing is causing some of these men to fantasize about being with you for intimate moments during the day. It will also cause them to think you want them to give you this attention.

If you're a happily married woman, it would not make sense to dress this way around hungry-minded men. They don't care about you being married, nor do they care about you having a boyfriend. So, what's the point? You can't have it both ways; you either respect yourself and, for others to do the same, you need to respect them as well by dressing appropriately. Well, you might say, "Even if I do dress appropriately, they are still going to give me a hard time." That may be true in some ways; however, it won't be because you are giving them excuses to do so; it would be because of the provocative ways you dress. The attention you would receive could be far less because of the respect you show from the way you present yourself. A woman who shows this kind of dress behavior has very little respect for her husband. If you're married, you shouldn't be advertising what your husband sees every night.

Single women who have a hard time finding good relationships may act this way in the workplace. However, even when they do, it shows just how low their self-esteem is. If you want a good man to respect you, you must first show him how much you respect yourself. Good women do not have to act like sleazy women who want men lusting after them. Later on, after you connect with him, he will show very little respect for you as a woman. If he found you acting like a whore then, he will later treat you like a whore because that is how you presented yourself to him. Good women should present themselves as a living sacrifice unto God, who will help you stay on the right track of being true to yourself. Ladies, the rights that everyone has been given here in America are not at all equal among men and women. Parts of society do not see you as having equal rights among men, some see you as sex objects, baby-makers, sex slave workers, and babysitters. However, there's still much to be done in fighting for the rights and respect for women.

Many workplaces do not allow relationships on the job due to conflict of interest. Often one partner would have to quit to fulfill the desires toward the other. That would be okay if the feelings between the two are mutual. Either way, a single good woman should remain on her guard while getting to know deeper levels of her co-worker. Remember, corrupt men are like wolves in sheep's clothing; you never know when the sleeper will awaken. It is not unusual for employees in the workplace to act friendly, helpful, and intelligent. It's what goes on in their personal lives when they leave the workplace that can be an eye-opener. Many police officers go home every night and beat up their wives, then go back on duty the next day as if everything is fine at home. Corrupt men all over the place hide behind their professions but, behind closed doors, they can be monsters to good women.

Small and large businesses employ corrupt-minded men without knowing it. The goal for employers in hiring new employees is to help grow the business. To generate new clients, employees should represent themselves as if they are the owners of the company by the way they treat the clients. When a company is productive, it stabilizes your position within the company. However, when corrupt men are employed by any company, it creates disruptive behavior for the women within the workplace. It could also be a stumbling block in growing new business for the company such as sexual harassment complaints, lawsuits against the company for not doing anything about it, and a high turnover due to unstable leadership. Companies that suffer from this type of problem have been promoting corrupt men to management and supervisory positions without seeing the big picture of who they really are.

Women who work in these types of environments have suffered a great deal of abuse. Many of the complaints from women who have been taken advantage of or abused in the workplace tend to be ignored by company owners, who themselves may be men. For generations, women have been on the short end of the stick when it comes to complaints filed within most companies. Good career women have quit good jobs due to sexual harassment behaviors. Their motivation, determination, self-esteem, and the joy and hope to better themselves have been crushed by the businesses that refuse to hear their cries for help. I believe this is one of the key reasons why women in Section I of this book act the way they do. They have stereotyped all men as having the same behavior toward women. Although most of us know that is not the case, it does kill many women's spirits to want to trust men to do right.

Ladies, you should focus on your strength and not your weakness. Use the power of righteousness while at the same time staying within the law. In other words, having the knowledge of Christ Jesus and believing that you can do all things through him gives you the power from within. When you stand your ground against the wilds of devilish men, our Lord and Savior will open doors to make things right while you're still trying to figure it out. You are not fighting against flesh and blood but against spiritual warfare within the workplace. Putting your faith and trust in God to help fight your battle will give you the peace and comfort needed to continue the fight. However, you will still need to follow through on filing your complaints and keeping notes on things that affect you by their corrupt behavior. You will eventually get heard by those that God chooses to hear your cries for help.

God can use any area of the law and anyone working within the law to be a blessing to you in times of need. So, I say to you, don't throw away your career or quit your job without a strong spiritual fight against those that have no respect and no morals or values to live by. Ladies, if you have any kind of foundation of truth in your life, know this: You are the greatest thing to yourself, other than God who created you. God did say you were created in the likeness of His image, which makes you one of His greatest creations. Don't cut yourself short by what evil men do to you; you have the power to cause evil men to lay at your feet. Faith in yourself and faith in God are powerful forces to be reckoned with. You must know that faith is the substance of things hoped for and the evidence of things not yet seen. You should be thankful in advance for what has not taken place yet, while knowing that your faith in God will come to fruition in due time.

Chapter 3

CLOSE ENCOUNTER CONVERSATIONS

Most people of the same sex very seldom stand close to the other person's face when holding a conversation. However, some men who are attracted to a woman they don't know well have an ulterior motive for wanting to stand directly in front of her face. If the woman is friendly and smiles a lot, it causes the unwanted creep to think that he's the reason for all that. He may slowly come upon you during a conversation just to get in your face for a closer encounter. He may want to smell you or put his hand on your shoulder in a lustful way. These can be ways he stimulates himself to do more and say more. To the woman, he's just being friendly and they don't see why he wants to get so close during their conversation. A woman who naïvely fails to see what's going on will cause the man to think she likes him and wants to spend more time with him. Not all men are this way; some are just outgoing and friendly. It's the in-your-face ones that you have to be careful of.

There are single and married men who have a way of interacting with women that goes beyond the way normal men would act. Keep in mind, ladies, these are men with corrupt ways of thinking about how they can satisfy themselves by getting to know you better. Up-close conversations can cause a man or a woman to lose him or herself in the other through small talk. This kind of behavior from a man or a woman could cause them to start saying things straight from their current thoughts about how they see each other. These are words they may be sorry they said later on or wish they had never shared those thoughts. Close encounters can put people in a different state of mind. It can cause you to think you know the person better than you do. For most corrupt men, this is exactly what they want a woman to think when in close contact. They want you to feel comfortable talking to them and being around them. The more they can get you to open up about yourself, the easier it is for them to steer you in the direction they are leading you.

A close encounter is also another way for them to see down your low-cut blouse. While you are focused on the conversation, he's focused on checking out what your boobs look like. He will smile, laugh, and make it look like he really enjoys being around you. Some women make the mistake of looking in a different direction when talking with men at close contact. It's okay to look away periodically but looking at him eye to eye will allow you to see what he's looking at while talking to you. Whenever a woman takes it for granted while being around men she doesn't know that well, she becomes the examining attention for many of those men. A woman can be in a public place, inside an office building, a store, or a mall, and she will be examined by the hungry eyes of men who enjoy fantasizing about what they can't have.

I am fully aware that many of you women will find

what I am saying hard to take in. That's because you probably never knew that men saw you in the way that I am sharing it with you. During many of my counseling sessions, I've had women tell me they didn't know men saw them in that way. This is also how some of them came to understand why they were being so abused sexually. There are husbands and single men who have a hard time seeing parts of their wife, or girlfriend's anatomy. These men can have an erection just looking at you, and will find it very difficult to continue whatever they were doing. You may not notice the behavior until he starts to become romantic with you after seeing you in your underwear or without your bra. Some women are aware that their mate can't control himself when she's walking around the house half-naked. However, if you're not in the mood and you know he's this way, you should keep certain areas covered if you don't want to be bothered having sex.

Some men are very sensitive to what they see on a woman. If you're married or have a boyfriend, these close encounters are natural; they are what strengthen the bond between the two. However, when a woman exposes part of her anatomy to men in public places outside or inside, she will find that some men want to get close to her. Some will even try to start a conversation with her, because their hormones are causing them to become excited and anxious. Men who act this way have strong sex drives and the desire to be satisfied as often as possible. Some women can't handle having sex three to five times or more a day; they become sore and uncomfortable. Because of this, many divorces take place because the man can't get enough of her.

There are all types of sex offenders in prisons today because of men who can't control their desire to be satisfied by women. Women are being kidnaped, little girls are being kidnaped, and even young boys are taken advantage of. These corrupt men will stop at nothing until they are caught red-handed. Ladies, that is why I am telling you these things; you need to know how you are looked at by these types of men. If you don't take note of what I am telling you, you may find yourself involved with a sex maniac who will sex you unconsciously. These are men who only care about satisfying themselves; they will throw you in the trash can when they are done with you.

Chapter 4

HOW YOU ARE BEING WATCHED

T here are men in our society today who are lurking in the dark places of their minds. It doesn't matter whether it's day or night, these men always hide themselves this way. When their animal instinct kicks in to find the right woman or girl, they will stalk you when you are unaware that you are being looked at. They will look at you in the same manner that the lions look at gazelles in the jungle. There are many to choose from but what they mostly look for is their weakness. Most jungle prey animals are very timid; they know, if they don't keep a good look-out for the enemy lurking after them, they will be eaten alive. Ladies, I'm not saying you need to act this way, I am only saying you need to keep your guard up when out in public places.

Be aware of your surroundings and try to know who's watching you. Some stalkers will follow you the whole time you're in public places; they are very patient when they have made up their minds to get what they want. Once you get in your car to head home, some will even trail you to your house to see where you live. If you live alone and they come into this knowledge, it will motivate them even more to try and catch you off guard. Millions of women, girls, and children around the world have had their humanity taken away from them to do the things no human should have to endure. Whenever there's a weather disaster and people become homeless, it is time for the criminal-minded corrupt men to pretend to want to help those in need.

These men will set up fake shelters to lure women and girls who have no place to go. They will do whatever it takes to gain your trust in them and, when they do, it will be for them to move you to where they can use you to make money in the sex industry. There are many heartless men in this world, men who have no conscience; they feel no guilt and they have no remorse for the wrong they do to women. When one human looks at another human in an inhumane way, they become predator animals among the human race of people. Ladies, unless you are married to a loving husband, someone who has proven his loyalty to you, trust no man. Some men will turn demonic on you when the right opportunity arises, then go back to being "Mr. Righteous" when there are witnesses in the area. They will threaten to harm or kill you if you tell anyone what they did to you and, in some cases, they will threaten your family.

Ladies, if you live in a big city with a large population of people, you can rest assured that predator men are watching and waiting for you to come down that lonely alley. Large cities have many hidden places to take women, who are snatched off the streets. If you're walking alone, you should be aware of these things. However, some women want to be seen as being tough around men and can take care of themselves. They go to places where they might in up being the only female; they then become trapped and unable to leave. Dozens of dogs in a fenced yard that haven't eaten for days will fight to the death over a T-bone steak. When a woman puts herself alone among men she doesn't know, she becomes, in some ways, that T-bone steak. Believe it or not, there are actually sick men among us who would love to literally eat parts of a woman's body. This is the extreme depths that a corrupt sick-minded man will go to satisfy his sexual desires.

I have much respect for women who truly respect themselves and will not cause men to lust after them by the provocative clothes they wear in public places. Ladies, if you don't want men watching every move you make, stop advertising the goods or you will get robbed from head to toe. When the robber takes as much as he can take from you, he would normally leave what he doesn't need any more on the side of the road or he'll throw it in the trash can, near the alleyway. Use common sense, ladies, read between the lines of what I am saying to you. To gain the wisdom, knowledge, and understanding concerning the things that could happen to you, trust not only in yourself but in God as well. He will guide and protect you in all that you do in life. It would be better for you to lean not on your own understanding, but in all your ways acknowledge Him and He shall direct your path.

Every woman has a right to be herself and dress comfortably when out and about. However, after reading this book and becoming fully aware of how special you are, you should want to take precautions, knowing that corrupt men are attracted to you. Of course, there are those of you who welcome the attention you get from men. But, when you take it for granted that they will give you the respect you deserve and some of them don't, things could turn really ugly. That's the time when you wished you had used better judgment. It may be fun having all those eyes watching you but, baby girl, let me tell you, when one of those dogs grabs your ABC without your permission and starts biting all over you from head to toe, just do what you're told and you might get away alive. However, if you're in an area where people would be able to hear your screams, do so if you think he might run away and if he's not using deadly force on you. Either way, you will have to make that call if you find yourself in one of those situations.

Chapter 5

WANTED AND UNWANTED ATTENTION

Most of us, if not all of us, are aware that babies demand attention when they want something. They will scream and holler until someone gives them the attention they demand. We give them that respect because we know they can't do it for themselves. This attention is given until the baby reaches a certain age and is taught to do some things for him or herself. As the child gets older, more and more is expected of them to do for themselves. The pattern of reducing the attention given continues until the child reaches its late teenage years, at which time the parents should have taught the young adult how to do for themselves. It should be common for parents to teach their children the basic common sense of how to live in this world. However, that is not always the case in many households. Young adults around the world are living life carelessly, in and out of different places.

Wanted attention is one thing, unwanted attention is another. Women who have not been taught the dangers that lie in this world are placing themselves in many dangerous situations. The continuation of wanting attention can be viewed in many different ways. One way is getting the public to see the need for helping people who lack the knowledge of how to help themselves. Another way can be trying to sell goods or an invention you have created to better the lifestyle of mankind. The list of reasons for wanting to get people's attention could go on and on. However, there are things about ourselves that we should not be trying to get people's attention for, especially from men with corrupt minds. I am aware that many women in this world have little understanding of the mindset of mankind and the things they can do to them. Women with this nonchalant attitude in many cases wake up in the wrong places or they don't wake up at all.

When you come into the knowledge of who you are and the things you know to be true in life, it gives you a greater edge over those who don't know you. Why? Because you now have a wider view of the things that are going on around you. This, in turn, causes you to become more careful as you travel through life's journey. Knowing what you know about yourself, along with the knowledge you've obtained and your common sense, can make or break you, depending on how you use it. If you're a woman who's self-centered and continues to accept attention that can be harmful to you, it would be just a matter of time before the pain of your behavior kicks in.

Women who understand what they have about themselves and reject receiving this type of attention will do whatever is needed to prevent being looked at inappropriately. Some men will act and give you unwanted inappropriate attention if you give them reasons to do so. Children who have no control over the unwanted attention they get should be protected by their parents. However, as an adult woman, you can't expect your boyfriend or your husband to be around all the time to protect you. The provocative ways you may dress when you're with your husband could also put him in danger. In today's society, a corrupt-minded man will use a weapon to silence your man and force you to go with him. So now, if that be the case, wouldn't it make sense to protect him and yourself from this crazy world of danger?

Being the man that I am, I would not have a woman hanging on my arm, looking like a slut from a back alley. Any woman who continues to show her ABC in public places while with her husband has no respect for her husband or her boyfriend. The boyfriend or husband who tolerates this type of woman who conducts herself this way has no true morals or values to live by. He is willing to let her reveal to the world what he sleeps with every night, how she maintains control over him, and the fear he has of losing her to someone else. Good ladies, I know most of you are much better than that. However, the ones who would get offended at what I just said are the ones from Section I of the book. They will scream the loudest because they don't want to be seen as low-life women. No one can deny a shoe that fits perfectly on both feet unless they want to change to a different style of shoe.

Speaking of change, ladies, if you are truly one of the women from Section I of this book, change is possible for you. Just accept that you have made mistakes in your life and are willing to repent of your sinful behavior. From this point, you should want to seek true guidance for your life.

There is only one person who ever lived a perfect life on planet earth, He is the only one who can truly give you the change you need; His name is Jesus Christ. He will never steer you wrong, his knowledge and benefits in helping you deal with problems are unlimited. Once you change from the old pair of shoes you're wearing to the new lifestyle pair, your walk in life will never be the same again. Your view of self and life will be different, you will see people for who they are, and you will find yourself being careful.

After you have settled into your new shoes, you will still have that desire to want attention to yourself. However, the attention that you want will be spiritual, meaning that you will want to have a closer relationship with Jesus as your Lord and Savior. To walk right in your new shoes, you most certainly want Him to be with you at all times. You might ask, "How do I do that?" By acknowledging Him in all that you do in life; you're going to need his support and protection wherever you go. You must understand that you will never ever be alone as you are walking in His presence. Although His spirit of truth, love, and righteousness will be inside you, you will be walking by faith, not by what you see in this life. Good women who know this are living peaceful lives without fear of the unknown.

The attention in this world can lead to pain and destruction if you go about it the wrong way. However, having the greater power that lives within you (Christ Jesus), He will steer you in the right way of how to do things without you creating problems for yourself. People will see you differently and will show more respect in the way they interact with you. The criminal-minded and corrupt behavior of men, who will try to see you disrespectfully, will be dealing with the greater power that is within you. God will reveal to you what is happening around you, he will also show you a way out of a bad situation.

Chapter 6

GETTING TO KNOW YOU

I n today's society, more and more people are getting to know each other through the media. It's not unusual for young women and girls to be impressed by the sweet words and nice sounds coming from men on the other end of their phone or computer— men they have never met. It is almost a thing of the past for people to introduce friends to other friends in person. Women all around the world are allowing themselves to fall in love online with men they have never met, even men who live in other states and other countries. What many of you women don't realize is that many of these men are corrupt, devious, and full of criminal behavior. They are fishing for women who are desperate, naïve, and very inclined to believe whatever they say. There are so many ignorant good women in this world who deserve to be treated with dignity and respect but, instead, are being trapped, used, and abused by the very men they thought they knew.

Ladies, you are such a jewel to all mankind; without you, we will not be able to increase in number. That is why you must understand that the more you know about man's behavior, the better you are at making the right decision when interacting with men. There is a day-and-night dif-ference between talking to a man on a website (whom you have never met or seen) and having that same conversation in person. The presence of a person tells a different story when talking to them. People react differently when they are not being truthful; especially when you are looking at them eye to eye. Your thinking process is not the same as it would be in talking to that person online. In person, you may want to know more about the person's background and what they are all about. Online, a person can get caught up by hearing sweet and kind words inside of a fun-filled conversation. You can get caught up in all the small talk and never think about who the person really is.

After so many days and weeks of communicating back and forth, you come to think you're in love with the guy, yet you know nothing about his background. In many cases, you may only see the person's face online while having all those conversations. Before you know it, he's asking you to meet him or he wants to come to your place and meet with you. This kind of dating has become a goal mine for corrupt men. Ladies, your female weakness becomes a free-for-all for anyone who wants a piece of you. The best tools they use are con words, in convincing you that they really care about you or that they've fallen in love with you. These kinds of men are pros at what they do to you; if they can get you to believe everything they say online, they can then control you in person. Don't let yourself become a puppet dangling by strings and controlled by corrupt-minded men. They will not only take you out for breakfast, lunch, and dinner just to keep you healthy and good-looking but may also share "you" as a meal for their friends, who may be waiting for you at another location.

Women who put all their trust in an online man after a short or long period and only obtain particles of information about him may put themselves in great danger only to suffer a rude awakening later on. These men are patient and will do whatever it takes to win you over in trusting them. That, my lady friends, is the key to their success and a slow death for you. They will butter you up so well, that you'll find yourself sliding down a pole with answers to every question they ask you, questions you shouldn't be answering about yourself; simply because you don't know enough about him. Your answers will give him a one-sided advantage over you. Their approach to young girls is a cakewalk, unlike young women, who may have had some experience with men, young girls are naïve in every way. Having a man talk to them online in a romantic way makes them feel like they are grown women and can handle themselves very well.

Sadly, many of these little girls end up missing after their first date with this kind of guy. That is why it is so important, ladies, for you to teach your daughters to not let the words of a man draw her into him. The internet has made it possible for girls to meet grown men who pretend to be young teens or young men close to their age. They are being targeted more so than grown women. Taking the internet away from them is not the answer; teaching them and having them read books like this will help open their young eyes to the real truth about men and boys. Women and girls who grew up abused and were never told how lovely they are or how much they are loved are the desperate ones, looking for love from the wrong people. Most women are affectionate and need to hear how much they are loved and needed by a man who really cares. Many of them will turn to the internet to find these satisfying answers through the men they meet online. However, the answers they find will later disappoint them in a devastating way.

The culture of women throughout the world is ever changing. They are becoming more susceptible to words from criminals that have no real meaning. Movie producers, TV shows, and private companies are exploiting women through the media in so many different ways. Their naked bodies have become a symbol of lust for all to see. It is becoming more and more common for women to think it's okay to feel comfortable dressed half-naked in public places. Ladies, you can't have it both ways if you know and have come to an understanding that some men are weak-minded when they look at parts of a woman's anatomy. Many of these corrupt-minded men will do their best to have a piece of you, and if you refuse, they're wanting to get to know you; they may take what they want from you at a later date or time. Their behavior is greatly stimulated by the provocative ways many of you dress in public places.

Therefore, it should not be surprising when you find yourself being raped so easily. If you're taken to a place out of public view, there is not much for them to take off you when they're trying to get to the goods. After it happens, you may file a complaint of rape and hope the rapist will get charged if he's caught. However, if you would dress appropriately, knowing that this could happen to you, it would lessen the desire for men to pay attention to you. You women who are good to yourself in understanding the danger that lies in this world, I salute you for being careful. Regardless of how much right you think you have in the way you dress around other people, other people may not see what one or two men are doing to you behind the scenes. Every person in society has rights and, when those rights are violated, you may find that, in a court of law, the judge may show more leniency toward the rapist than you. You might ask why. The details of what you were wearing before the rape will be taken into consideration by lawyers and court judges. In most of these cases, men are handling the case.

Please don't think that judges and lawyers are people that can do no wrong. Many of them have lustful thoughts in the same manner as corrupt-minded men. That is one of the reasons that so many women who try to fight these cases come out on the losing end of the stick. So, ladies, you must understand that the law says you can do certain things and dress certain ways in society but it does not say that you will be safe in doing it. It only gives you the right to do it; it is up to you to be careful for yourself. The law in this society is just as corrupt as some of the criminals on the streets. From 2016 to the end of 2020 and on into January of 2021, we came close to being a lawless nation, based on what was happening in Washington, D.C. So, ladies, make no mistake, your rights will not protect you from criminal corrupt-minded men. Rather than letting everyone else get to know all about you, take so time to get to know yourself; before you become a victim in this society. Understand what you can do for yourself, to stay safe from the dangers that surround us.

Chapter 7

MISCONCEIVED CONVERSATIONS

I t is so easy for some men to misinterpret what a good-looking woman is saying to them. The smile on her face, along with her movements, causes them to see her differently from what she might be saying. As I have said earlier in other chapters, the look, smell, and proximity of certain women can cause a mental fantasy with some men while communicating. Some women can be very sociable, playful, and talkative with men, even if they're married or have a boyfriend. This behavior can cause some men to misread what the woman is saying. Some men will take it as flirting with him and or wanting him to like her. In many cases, good women who had no desire of getting involved end up giving in to the attention being shown by the man.

There are many reasons women conduct themselves this way. Those that are married may have a husband that is in the military or he's working in a foreign country. Other reasons could be related to factors such as diabetes, high blood pressure, or other medical problems that can cause a husband to become impotent, unable to achieve a sexual erection. This can cause some women to act much differently around single men or even other married men. Their desire to be sexually satisfied causes them to draw a great amount of attention to themselves when talking to men. Men can almost sense when a woman is not receiving sexual attention at home to keep her satisfied and more relaxed when she's around friends. Some of these men will jump at the opportunity of giving her the pleasures she needs. These are men who will drop any morals or values they hold for relationships just to take advantage of an easy catch.

Most women who have husbands or boyfriends that are unable to fulfill their sexual commitment may truly love them but may not be aware of how they are conducting themselves around other men. They want to be faithful but the hunger for sex and to be satisfied causes them to fantasize about other men. This desire and attention affect nearly every man who knocks on her door and the ones she knows as a friend. We often hear of women sleeping with the postman, the milkman, the repairman, and even the garbage man. Believe it or not, most of these women are very good to their husbands and are truly trying to do their best; to stay faithful within the relationship. However, because of their weakness, these men can see right through them; and will make it easy for her to have them.

Many children in our society are unaware that their father is not their natural father, yet these men who are unable to satisfy their wives have accepted raising the child. Some of these men don't want to lose their good woman and understand that her needs are not being met at home. However, in other cases, many divorces have taken place due to this type of behavior. Couples who deal with the issue of not being sexually satisfied can be taught how to satisfy their partner in other ways. Some men who can't sexually perform in satisfying their wife will not bother doing anything if they themselves can't be satisfied. That, in and of itself, is wrong; even if he can't be satisfied, he should not cause his wife to suffer the desire to be. If a man truly wants to keep his wife from wanting other men, he should sacrifice by pleasing her in every other way to make her feel loved by him as a man. There are many things on the market that give ways of pleasing your partner; there should not be excuses for anyone not being able to satisfy the need in making love to their wife or husband.

The same can be said about a woman who has no desire to be sexually penetrated by her man. This could be due to great pain or a medical issue that may prevent her from having intercourse. However, women should know that, if you have a man who is fully functional and desires to be satisfied, you as a woman should make it happen in other ways. Remember, if you're a woman trying to please your husband and you truly love him, it should not be a handicap that you can't or don't want to perform because you can't be satisfied. You would be putting him in the same position as a woman with a husband who is sexually impotent: causing him to look at other women with lust and a desire to be satisfied. Men and women who suffer from the issue of not being satisfied will, in most cases, read the opposite sex (during conversation) the wrong way. Couples who have been together for many years may find themselves unable to perform with their partner due to medical or other reasons.

Whole families are destroyed due to outside extra affairs with other people just to satisfy sexual needs. As long as the affair is kept secret and both parties involved understand that it's just to satisfy the need, it will keep happening until the truth is discovered. Once everything comes to light and you can no longer hide the secret, the people who will suffer the most will be the children, if there are any. The next person will be your husband or wife who did not try to satisfy you. There will be anger, sorrow, and wishing that more could have been done to prevent it from happening. Some of these people are churchgoers; they spend so much time in the church that they lose sight of the fact that they have a spouse at home that needs their attention. The wisdom of man is foolishness before God. When a person thinks his walk with God and the things they do in a church building are more important than satisfying spouse or family, they are putting themselves on a pedestal for a great fall. Pastors, deacons, evangelists, and other church leaders need to wake up and put family first before putting themselves on a pedestal.

Great work is done before God when a person is in tune with what is going on at home. Cleaning up other people's houses when your own house is starving for love in all the right places will not look good in God's sight. A satisfying relationship sets a growing example for children seeing how it should be done. Ladies, if you're acting in ways that cause men to misread you during conversation, stop and think of how you can help your husband help you achieve satisfaction. Try your best to convince him to seek a counselor who understands how to communicate his need to help meet your needs. If he can't find one, have him read this book, then have him contact me on my website for an online counseling appointment if needed.

Chapter 8

UNEXPECTED OR UNWANTED GIFTS

Women who have outgoing personalities and are overfriendly tend to get feedback from men in many different ways. A man may surprise you by sending you flowers or a box of chocolates because he may think you are interested in him. It may not have been your intention of misleading him to believe such a thing; nonetheless, it happens. When I was seventeen years old, I went to a church with my older sister and she saw a good friend of hers who waved at her as a gesture of saying "Hi." I had never met the girl, yet she looked so beautiful to me. She was a teen in the same age group as me and we sat four rows behind her. She saw me next to my sister and turned back around and began waving at me. I looked behind me to see who she was waving at, not realizing she was looking at me. When she did get me to look in her direction, I realized she was looking at me and I excitingly waved back. As I sat there throughout the service, the only thing I could think of was this beautiful girl waving at me. After church, I got her name from my sister and she talked with us a short bit before leaving.

She was very friendly and somewhat outgoing with my sister. I did not know at the time that she had a boyfriend in another state. However, I was determined to get to know this doll of a girl if it was the last thing I did. I managed to get her phone number to build friendship and from there I pursued, getting her to let me date her. I bought gifts, took her out to the movies, and many other things took place. After a few months of dating, she finally came clean and told me she had a boyfriend in another state. Today, when I look back on what she did then, it tells me that she was lonely and needed companionship. Her boyfriend was too far away to give her that. I pursued her because of her frantic desire to get my attention at a church, thinking that she wanted me to get to know her better. Ladies, if you're receiving gifts from men whom you never got to know that well, it's only because you may have unintentionally led him to believe you wanted his attention.

If you have a good marriage or have a boyfriend that's treating you right, you should let that person know what your status is and that it wasn't your intention for him to think that you were single and free. It can be a dangerous thing for a woman to allow a man to think she is single and free to date him. You may be lonely and in need of affection from your mate, which you may not be getting. However, to mislead another man by allowing him to buy you gifts and to do other expensive things for you would be wrong. When the truth is finally revealed, it could cause a great deal of trouble for you and your spouse. Some men will not let go so easily and may want revenge for what you did to them.

Men today are more unpredictable than ever, especially when it comes to spending money on a woman they thought they were building a relationship with. Good women are caught in a love triangle they never knew existed; the love of their husband or boyfriend and a man who assumed she likes him because of her friendly behavior toward him. He may have fallen in love with her and sent gifts anonymously. These cases do exist because some men do not know how to fully express themselves in person. Not knowing her status, they will send gifts and other things in the hope that she will know who it is that is sending them. There are, however, those men who will know your status of being involved with someone else and will not care one way or the other. They will still send you gifts to get your attention. This is called an obsession with the determination to get positive feedback.

If the problem is not stopped before getting out of control, it can lead to a gridlock situation without your permission. This type of person may have ulterior motives for wanting to have you. It is not uncommon for married women or women in strong relationships with boyfriends to suddenly get snatched up by slave traders for money. Men with corrupt behaviors come in many different shapes, sizes, colors, attitudes, personalities, and professions. Just when a woman thinks she knows a person well, she ends up with a bag over her head, tied up, and sold for money. Accepting gifts from men when you're already in a relationship is like playing Russian roulette with one bullet in the chamber, hoping that your mate or spouse never finds out who's sending the gifts or being willing to lie and say it's from a distant family member. Regardless of how much you may like the gift, it spells trouble either way you look at it.

Gifts should be kept only when the two people have mutual feelings toward each other or if it is a farewell gift of breaking up to date other people. This type of giving shows a clear understanding of what is expected of each other. Unwanted and unexpected gifts should never be accepted without a clear understanding of the intentions for the gift. If the intentions are wrong, the right decision should be made to stop the misconception of misleading thoughts from past conversations. Ladies, there's a right way and a wrong way to interact with men who don't know you. Men are naturally attracted to you and more so if he finds interest in you because of your looks or the way you're shaped. Your overfriendly behavior will cause him to think you're an easy catch and he'll want to know more about you. Unless you want this type of attention, you should be careful of this type of feedback; it could bite you on your butt later on.

Chapter 9

HIDDEN SECRETS

Men who have the ulterior motive of using you will spend a great deal of money trying to get to know you better. However, that's not to say that good men with good intentions don't spend money; on the contrary, it depends on the interest of the man and what's in it for him. Although, in today's society, men and women tend to not want to know right away who their partner really is. They are too anxious about getting into bed with each other just to taste the goods to see what it is like with him or her. Ladies, I must say, that is not a good idea; you must keep in mind that you are the ones who can have babies. No child should be born in this world not knowing who his father is. That has been the case for many generations and is still happening today. There are many men in our society who consider themselves to be playboys and their whole goal is to have a good time with easy-going women. They will sweet-talk you into the bedroom to get their rocks off and then, after many weeks and months of the good times, they will leave you high and dry. If you happen to get pregnant, you can rest for sure he may call you a slut because you slept with him the first night you met him. In his mind, who's to say you haven't done it with other men like him.

Ladies, don't get labeled as a prostitute by men who are not willing to get to know you better. The worst thing you could do to yourself is end up with three to five children, each having a different father. We all see it happening every day with young mothers who think with their legs open for more of the same. You cannot leave it up to the man to make decisions for you when it comes to sleeping with him. If you haven't done a background check of what he's all about and who he really is, you may get left carrying a baby for nine months. When a man like this meets you for the first time, he's scoping you out, he's looking for a weakness to get into your world. That weakness could be your over-friendly behavior and answering personal questions more quickly; which gives him more insight into who you are. Women who are lonely and in need of companionship will in many cases act this way with men. I am not saying it's wrong to be over-friendly; you just need to be more aware of corrupt-minded men as they communicate with you.

You as a woman should know your weakness and think before answering personal questions some men may ask you. If you're looking for a good man, take charge and be in control of asking the questions you need to know. In doing this, you will be forcing him to show his hand at what he's all about. If he fails to answer certain questions, a red flag should go up. This should let you know that the guy is not being honest with you or he's afraid you may find out what he's really about. Ladies, never let a man see how desperate you are for companionship; focus on your strength and not your weakness. He will surely know upfront that a one-night stand with you is not happening. Getting to know each other over a period of time will allow you to see how much he respects you. If you are being pushed to have sex in a short period, you should be aware that it may not be about building a relationship with you, but more about having sex for pleasure.

Companionship is long-lasting and it does not focus on one thing. It's all about love, which has no boundaries: *"Love suffereth long, and is kind; love envieth not; love vaunteth not itself, is not puffed up, Doth not behave itself unseemly, seeketh not her own, is not easily provoked, thinketh no evil; Rejoiceth not in iniquity, but rejoiceth in the truth; Beareth all things, believeth all things, hopeth all things, endureth all things. love never faileth."* You can find more of these attributes of love in 1 Corinthians 13:4-13 KJB. Ladies, if the man you're getting to know, or have been with for some time, does not show these attributes toward you, regroup to find out what it is he wants from you. A relationship should be built on all the things concerning true love toward each other. The key is taking your time by asking the right questions and getting a better understanding of who he is and why he wants to be with you.

If you're newly dating someone and he gets upset when you ask questions that hit a nerve, ask him what's causing him to get upset. If he refuses to answer but instead threatens to break up with you because you keep asking too many questions, let him break up with you. Hidden secrets can be devastating in a relationship later on, especially toward women from men. Ladies, don't cave in and stop asking because of his threats to leave; stand your ground and watch how he may cave in and tell you a lie just to keep you from leaving. If the answer you hear from your question is a quick response, rest for sure it's a lie. You should have him articulate his answer in more detail, so you get a better understanding for your question.

A lady who had been married for nearly forty years and had been divorced for nearly ten years came to me for counseling. The problem was the anger her oldest daughter had toward her in recent months. Before she got married to her husband, she had been one month pregnant with another man's baby. She said she did not know at the time that she was pregnant and later married the man who acted as father not only to the child that wasn't his but four other children, as well. He thought all five children were his children. After the divorce and the kids were all grown and some married, the oldest daughter's real father found out where she lived. She was thirty-eight years old and never knew any other father but the one who raised her. This man called her and explain how her mother left him for another man while being pregnant with her. They took a DNA test to prove the facts and the results tore the daughter up with anger. Not only did the daughter not know, but her stepdad never knew as well.

Hidden secrets may not show up in the beginning but I can assure you that, somewhere along the line in life, the truth will be revealed. If you're a young woman and in the limelight of dating, stop and think about what you've just read above. You could destroy your children with this kind of devious behavior. Being a mother without a good man can be very hard in raising children. Respect yourself and make sure the man you're with respects you and is willing to be with you through thick and thin. That young man you are dating might have two or more kids by other women that you may not be aware of. That is why I keep saying that you should ask the right questions and take your time on getting to know him better. The decisions you make today (good or bad) can hunt you for the rest of your life. Love yourself first, then see yourself as the greatest thing to yourself, other than God, who created you. If you can do that, men and other people will see you with the same respect with which you see yourself.

Chapter 10

SHOWING GOOD MANNERISM

S ome of the best actors in society are people who pretend to be what they never were. These are men and
women who can fool the very elect in every area of
society. However, my focus will be on the men who can
fool some women into thinking they are truly Mr. Right.
They can do this by the way they conduct themselves, how
well they communicate with you, their proper behavior
around you, their desire to assist you when you need help
with something, showing sympathy toward you during bad
situations, and making themselves available whenever you
call. These are men who put their true identity to sleep in
order to be what a woman wants them to be. Some of these
men can only hold their acting position for so long before
waking up to their true selves. This means that, if they have
not achieved what they are after within a certain time, they
tend to lose patience with you and become the person you
never knew. We all see it in the courtrooms every day, a
boyfriend or husband who beat a wife or girlfriend to death
over things that amount to nonsense.

It is so important for a woman to take her time when
it comes to building a relationship with a man she may be
attracted to. The more time you give yourself, the more you
will be able to see who he really is behind the scene. A per-

son can only hold their breath for so long; men who lock themselves on the inside are fighting to get out; they want to be themselves. However, they know if they come out too soon, they will surely lose you. Ladies, you have everything to gain in life and nothing to lose by letting a pretender go his way. Good manners come naturally for most people but can be hard for men who are corrupt-minded. They are men who are self-centered in every way and will cut you down if they can't get what they want or if you get in their way. Men like this are looking for women who are attractive and easygoing, have good jobs, and make plenty of money or come from a wealthy family and stand to inherit a large portion of land, money, or business. Although it doesn't matter what type of woman she may be; it all depends on how much knowledge she has about the behavior of men. This knowledge will help her see through all the demeanors he shows up front, only to see the real wolf on the inside.

A weak-minded woman who is ignorant about the behavior of these kinds of men will fall prey in most cases. These men are clever and smart and can be very patient with you when they understand your weakness. If you're a woman doing well for yourself and are determined to be successful at achieving your goals in life, follow your heart and stay on track. However, if you're looking for a good man to share that success with, be patient, be mindful, be careful, be very inquisitive about who he is, and stay alert for changes in his behavior. If you do this, you will sell smoothly at achieving all your goals in life. Why? Because you will be maintaining control of your personal goals in life without the interruption of a corrupt-minded man.

Remember, a self-centered man who starts out being nice to you, after seeing how hard you're working to achieve your personal goals, will try to turn your hard work into doing it for him. How? By making you feel that his career goals are more important than yours and that he can make more money for the both of you if you help him achieve his goals first. These situations often happen when two people are married and with some couples who may have been dating for many years. In many cases, the man will persuade you to put your own goals on the back burner to help him achieve his goals. Once he has obtained his goals and is making the big money you helped him achieve, he then leaves you for the woman he's been dating in the last year of his goal completion. Does that sound familiar to some of you ladies reading this book, or maybe you know someone to whom this has happened? Nonetheless, you need to stay focused on what you know is right for you.

If a man is not as focused as you on achieving his goals in education, career, or starting a business, and he is looking for you to help him in doing so, you should tell him to go back home to his mom and dad; that is, if he's your boyfriend. However, if the man is your husband, you should try to work together in supporting each other's efforts of being successful together. Uncommitted relationships can fall through the cracks at any time. A woman staying with a man while unmarried to him and supporting him in this way can be in for a rude awakening later on. Your kindness in helping him could be "appreciated" by him leaving you for another woman. After you've spent thousands of dollars supporting his dreams and goals, and the unexpected happens, it would be almost too late to say it was a loan to him. People shacking up together and acting like a married couple do not have much ground to stand on when things go wrong.

Most court cases will tell you that, unless you can prove that it was a loan made to him and he agreed to pay you back, there's not much they can do to help you. Ladies, you must understand that this kind of man will be very kind, nice, and loving to you, as long as you are supporting his wants and needs. If you change gears in the middle of the game, you will see signs of change in his attitude toward you. In other ways, he may sugarcoat you with sweet words of how you are such a blessing at helping him achieve his goals. He will use different methods to try and get you back on track of supporting his needs. It would be easy for many young women, wet behind the ears, to fall for a man like this, with this type of behavior. Try to achieve your own goals first before giving all your eggs to someone else.

Chapter 11

DATING A LAZY MAN

The attitude of some men toward women has changed a lot over the generations. More men are looking for a woman to take care of them instead of it being the other way around. More doors are opening up to women in the same fields of work as for men, which creates a great deal of competition with men competing for the same jobs. Men who find themselves on the lower end of the income bracket are more apt to date women with higher-paying jobs than themselves. There's nothing wrong with that, as long as the man truly loves the woman and wants to build success together. A great deal can be achieved with two good incomes working together. A couple with a true feeling of love toward each other can achieve much: a nice home, nice lifestyle, and many other joyful things that can take place; when working as one couple together.

There are many young single women attending college, working toward a better life for themselves. Many of these women happen to run into men at the same school who are working toward their own goals in life. I see this as a good thing for people who want to better themselves, while at the same time seeing other people with the same mindset. Ladies, dating a man who is setting a high bar for himself, as to what you are doing as well, is a good thing. Why? Because you have a good idea of where this guy is heading in life. The fact that you both are working toward similar goals will make it much easier to communicate with him about future planning.

There are many possible downfalls and consequences when dating a man who has no plans in life. You may never meet these kinds of men in college because many of them are too busy living off other people. They may work jobs here and there but are not stable enough to take care of themselves. These are men who will dress up and pretend to be what they never are and never were. They will try to impress you with lies about themselves just to get you to date them. A woman who has no experience with men may fall for this and pay a heavy price later. Ladies, in the same way that a whore stands on the street looking ever so enticing to men, causing them to lust after her, lazy men are doing the same thing to you. However, many of them are not standing on the street corner waiting for you, they are out looking for you. They will do anything humanly possible to convince you that they are the right guy for you. If you can't see the fruits or the potential fruits of the man's labor among all the things he's saying to you, he's deceiving you.

Many signs indicate what a lazy man is all about, signs you will see long before you get deeply involved with him. However, if you allow yourself to fall for his hypnotic spell over you, you will not see these signs. I am going to point out for all women, the signs to look for before dating any man.

Many Bible verses will tell you about these types of men who are good for nothing. I will only give you two book chapters and a couple of verses and then I will break it down to you on what it all means. *"He becometh poor that dealeth with a slack hand: but the hand of the diligent maketh rich. He that gathereth in summer is a wise son: but he that sleepeth in harvest is a son that causeth shame."* Proverbs 10:4-5 KJV *"In all labour there is profit: but the talk of the lips tendeth only to penury."* Proverbs 14:23 KJV

Men who go through life not wanting to get their hands dirty will depend on others to provide for them. They want the benefits of what life has to offer but are not willing to raise a hand to make it happen. The more you do for him, the less he wants to do for himself or for you. This is because he may see your weakness as wanting to help him. It doesn't matter what your needs or desires are; he will not show one bit of concern for you because it's all about him and not you. If he thinks you are on to his lazy way of behaving, he will come up with every excuse in the book to stop you from not wanting to be with him. If you try to get him to meet you halfway, he may lie just to appease you but will not act on anything he says. Dating a lazy man is like taking care of your little brother, who is already being taken care of by your parents. The only difference is that he's a grown man desiring the benefits of sleeping with a woman and still wanting the parent-like treatment to continue in his life. A man like this will ruin your career and cause you to regret ever meeting him.

The desires and temptations of wanting companionship can be very strong in some women. These thoughts and feelings can cause you to lose yourself in a man who may not be right for you. Taking your time and focusing on your personal goals can take that desire away temporarily. I would say the best way to move forward in achieving success is to crystallize your thinking with Christ as your guiding light. Determine what specific goal you want to achieve and then dedicate yourself to its attainment with unswerving singleness of purpose. Another thing I would suggest is to develop supreme confidence in yourself, God, and your own abilities. Enter every activity without giving mental recognition to the possibility of defeat. Concentrate on your strengths, instead of your weaknesses, on your powers, instead of your problems. In doing this, you can rest for sure that it will be very hard for corrupt-minded lazy men; to break through your barriers of determination. Ladies, keep your head up and know that you do not have to settle for second best; you deserve the best.

Chapter 12

WHO DO YOU PUT YOUR TRUST IN?

I n today's society, a man is only as good as his actions and that could go either way, good or bad. What a man might consider right may be wrong before God and those that believe in His truth. If two people are not walking on the same side of the street when it comes to decisions made in life, they are divided. Two minds that continue to be divided minds may never see the success that life has to offer nor the true joy and happiness they could have together. A strong-minded woman and a strong-minded man living together is a disaster waiting to happen. Why? If there's no real leadership, understanding, cooperation, and love between the two, they are just using each other to get what they want. God did put man in charge of all His creation on planet earth; however, if man fails to do the job right or doesn't do it at all, a woman has every right to pick up the baton, take control of her destiny, and run with it.

Ladies, unless that man has proven to you that he can be trusted and is willing to be with you through thick and thin, trust not only in him but put all your trust in God, Who gives life. Having a relationship with God through Christ Jesus will give you an inside look at the hidden things you were unaware of. Without spiritual knowledge from God, many things can go wrong. The man himself should be setting the example as head of the household by asking God to give him the wisdom to be a good husband and to lead in a loving way. Every person will have to answer to God for themselves for not standing on his truth and righteousness.

Mankind himself, being created in the image of God, was at one time perfect in every way. But his choice to be the tail and not the head in the Garden of Eden caused us all to be untrustworthy at times. We have all had a taste of what it means to be lied to and to lie to each other. Every person on the planet has at some point been disappointed by another person. We are all vulnerable to being lied to at certain points in our lives. The problem with that is this: Putting all your trust in man will disappoint you every time. For many women, when this happens, it destroys their entire world. Why? Because they had no backup to fall on. This is why it is so important to have that spiritual wisdom, knowledge, and understanding from God, Who will reveal to you the hidden things that a lying man will not tell you. Open your heart and your mind to His truth and He will never disappoint you.

I used to think that I was the only one that I could truly trust, other than God who created me. However, over the many years of living in this world, I have disappointed myself many, many times. Why? Because I am not perfect and neither are you. Ladies, you need that extra man on the inside to guide you through life's difficulties. All of my life Jesus has been my counselor, my lawyer, my doctor, my friend, my mom, my dad, my advisor, and, most of all, my Savior from the dangerous people in this world. To any woman, a man can be the biggest monster walking around on planet earth. Make no mistake, ladies, a guy can whisper in your ears all the sweet nothings you love to hear, then he'll turn around and cut you up and feed you to his dogs. We all know it, and we all have seen it in the news time and time again, the atrocities being done to women of all ages. Ladies, of all the chapters in this book, this is one you really need to imbed in your mind: "Who do you put your trust in?" When you understand who you are, and what it is going to take, to get you through life's daily struggles; you can then go through life without the fear of the unknown.

Chapter 13

BUILDING GOOD FRIENDSHIP

We often see people meeting in bars, clubs, civic centers, recreational centers, and even in churches. There are, however, many other places where people may meet for the first time. A person's character and personality can cause another person to feel like they have known that person for many years. Building friendships with people can be very warming as well as exciting. Interacting with people for the first time can open the doors to many opportunities. Everyone has different needs and wants, and connecting with the right people can possibly open those doors. The problem with that is this: Too often people who are losers will put themselves on top of a pedestal, making themselves out to be more than what they are. You will find this behavior a lot in some men who are looking for women to fall for them. It is not a good idea to fall for everything you hear from any man. Good women too often drop their guard over what some men will say in order to become friends with them.

Building friendship should not be an overnight thing; it needs time to materialize itself in many ways. We often tell our children that they should never get into a car with a stranger, yet many women who know this will do just the opposite themselves. Looking to become friends with a good man is not based on just what he says about himself. You should look at the overall picture of who he is and what he's truly about. Building a good friendship should take time and patience, especially on the woman's side. Getting to know the person you may like being around can answer many questions later on in life. You may later find that he can become very violent when provoked about certain things. His past relationships may have been unstable or you may find that he likes dating two or three women at the same time.

Believing everything a man says at the first meeting and shortly after becoming friends, without giving yourself time to see the bigger picture of what he's about, can become a disappointing factor in the days to come. The previous chapter talked about trust. A real friend is someone who is heartfelt, someone you can truly trust and depend on in times of need. However, these heartfelt thoughts and feelings should not come over a short period of days simply because you need companionship. In the same way you get people to earn your respect, it should be the same in building friendship. A man should prove himself worthy to be your friend and or companion. It should not be based on what he wants you to believe about him. If that becomes the case, it only means you are a desperate woman who is willing to believe anything. There are many good women out there who are very easy-going and will not put up a real fight about letting the man think they are friends.

It's okay for a woman to want to be friends with a man she has met for the first time. However, she should always use caution and not let that man think she has accepted his friendship. Ladies, let him prove to you how badly he wants to be your friend. He may ask for your phone number; tell him you'll think about it or you're not ready to go to that level just yet. Don't allow yourself to dance to his music, make him know that you're not desperate for his friendship. When you do balance your reaction to his desires, you're letting him know he's going to have to do more than just talk about himself. You want him to prove who he is and what he's about. There are many ways you can allow yourself to keep in touch with him. However, the thing you are saying to him is: "I am in control of who I let into my world." A good woman who shows much respect for herself and demands the same respect from any man who wants to be her friend will, in most cases, attract men who will respect her.

Society is full of good women who have become friends with monsters in sheep clothing. This has taken place because many of you don't give yourself the right balance in your decision-making. I spent five years living and working in South Korea; it took me nearly seven months to acclimate to the lifestyle, culture, and behavior of the people. I now have friends all over Korea. Why? Because I took my time in getting to know the people; and the way they operate. You don't have to go to a foreign country to understand what it means to acclimate to another person's world. People all over America are trying to better understand each other as friends at different levels of life. Making friends with men is almost the same as acclimating to his world of truth and lies. My morals and value system were day-and-night different from how the Koreans operate. I said that to make this point: a man's world may never measure up to your world as a woman.

It is always better to keep your defense shields up so you won't get harmed by his actions and or his behavior. In doing so, it would not be a surprise to you, because you would not have allowed yourself to get too close in thinking that you know him. Being a good friend does not mean putting all your trust in that person. Friends will always disappoint you time and time again. I have said this in earlier chapters: The best friend you could ever have, and one that will never ever leave you nor disappoint you is Christ Jesus, our Lord and Savior. When you find yourself at a loss for words to say to any man, Christ will direct your thoughts as to what to say, what to do, when to do it, and how to do it. He will also answer your call when you need His help. In the same way you converse with other friends, you can also talk to Him in the same manner but with respect.

Chapter 14

RESPECTING YOURSELF
TO GAIN RESPECT

Unlike men, women have a natural and unique way of attracting men unaware when in public places. "How?" you might ask. The way you are built, how you look, what you're wearing, how you smell, and the sound of your voice. What seems natural and normal to you is a turn-on for many devious-minded men who fantasize about having you in their clutches. For those of you who live in houses or apartments, understand the importance of the security needed to protect you. You have locks on your doors and windows to keep burglars and thieves from breaking in on you. This is especially important to you because you don't want to be caught off guard when you're in your bed sleeping at night. Any woman who is cognizant of the danger that lies in this world knows what she must do to protect herself when inside her home.

Ladies, the body you're living in is your temple away from that physical house you live in. So, if you have a great concern for protecting the place where you physically live; you should also be concerned about how you protect your body when you leave your house. People who live in your neighborhood don't know what's in your house. If someone knew you had something of great value stored there;

they might try to break in and still it. How much of your body you show in public places reveals to corrupt-minded men what they can take from you; if the right opportunity opens up to them. Revealing much of your anatomy in public places is giving rapists and sex slave bosses an opportunity to take away your humanity.

"I have every right to dress however way I want," you might say! Yes, you do, but if you have any concerns for your safety and don't want to be attacked; do the right thing. Corrupt-minded men have no respect for you or any other women who may dress respectably. However, when you open the windows to yourself, it causes these men to give you the most attention than the one who does protect herself out of concern. Ladies, each time you walk away from your house into the public, you cannot expect everyone to give you the respect you feel you should have. There are people (especially corrupt men) in this world who have no respect for anyone. Everywhere you go, someone is waiting to try and take away your human rights. It is important for every woman to be careful. Why? Because you were created to be a special woman; and you need to understand why you are being so targeted.

There are many younger and older women who are currently struggling with the trauma that took place when they were attacked and raped. Some of these women may have had great respect for themselves in the way they dressed in public places. However, the one who left the windows and doors wide open gave more reasons for their attackers to target them. In most of these cases, these women never thought this sort of thing could ever happen to them, which is one of the leading causes of many women being in these situations. They put too much focus on their right to do whatever makes them feel good. They don't think about the danger they put themselves in until some crazy man grabs them and takes away their rights to freedom.

Many women in our society want to prove to men that they are just as capable of doing the same job as a man and in some ways better. You may gain the respect of some men for what they see you can do. However, if you don't show them the respect they need to see of you being a woman around them and to yourself; they will not give you the respect you deserve as a real woman in their world. Proving you can do the job is one thing but dressing provocatively around them is asking for trouble. A woman who acts like a woman and wants to be the woman that God has created her to be is one of the most beautiful humans on the planet. Not every woman acts like a woman; many want to be as tough as a man, which takes away much of their femininity. The same can be said of men wanting to act like women, losing themselves in what they were never created to be. However, we won't go there; that behavior is for a different book. The goal right now is to help you see the jewel that you are as a beautiful woman on the inside. It doesn't matter what you look like on the outside, it is what you have on the inside and how you conduct yourself on the outside that appeals to most men. Staying focused on who you are, how much attention you draw to yourself, and being careful is among the most important things you need to know.

A normal family raising children will teach them respect early on in life as they grow. They set examples by closing the doors when bathroom needs are being met and when changing clothes in another room, away from other family members. These are just some of the ways children are taught to respect themselves. However, as adults, you may see people who are doing the opposite of what they may have been taught not to do in public places. This means that many women get caught up in what the world is doing and think that it's okay to do the same. This is where so many good women lose respect for themselves; they are following the path of the world and not the good morals and values taught by their parents based on the word of God. The world cannot and will not save you if you're locked up in a room, waiting to satisfy dozens of men's sexual desires, in a foreign country; and nobody knows where you are. That, my lady friends, can be the worst nightmare you'll never want to have. If you stay true to God, Who created you, and to yourself, you should not have to worry, instead, be careful and respectable.

Chapter 15

WHEN YOUR SPACE IS BEING INVADED

The work I do as a career counselor has taught me a lot of things about myself. Whenever I'm in public places or even indoors around people, I find myself observing behaviors all around me. I'm unaware of this most of the time; it has become second nature and a natural thing for me to conduct myself this way. When I'm counseling people, I am in a constant mode of monitoring and observing their reactions, behaviors, and attitudes to the questions I ask concerning their problems. The knowledge I've obtained over the years through this practice has given me a quick insight into the behavior of people like this. When I see their strange and unreasonable behavior toward other people in public places, it tells me what they are all about. This chapter will help you better understand why men stand closer to women than to men when communicating.

Whether you're on the street or inside a building, when some men approach a woman to talk, they tend to get less than one foot from their face. However, when they are talking to the same sex, they tend to stand further apart. Some women may not be aware of this behavior, but I do believe a great number of you are. For some men, this may just be a friendly way of communicating with the opposite sex, which may be how they have grown up in interaction with female family members. Some of these men are unaware that they may be offending you by invading your space. For these men, there is a nice way to gesture that they are too close, by raising your arm in front of them to show the distance you feel more comfortable with. Most will smile and understand, and some may even apologize for being too close.

It can be very uncomfortable for some women to have their space invaded by a man trying to get all in their face. Some of these men see this and know it but they will ignore how you feel just to get what they want out of it. Some will even raise their arm to put on your shoulder, pretending to be friendly. Believe it or not, ladies, some of these men are giving themselves a sexual fantasy high by imagining themselves being with you. It can be triggered by being inches from your face and/or the hand on your shoulder. To some of you women, this may sound crazy but I tell you the truth. I have worked with these kinds of people who live in fantasy worlds and they get their thrills from doing these sorts of things. Depending on where you are, this could be dangerous and could cause unexpected things to happen to you.

For example, you may be parked in a shopping area with a van next to your car or on your way back to your car from shopping, when a man with a map walks up to you pretending to be lost. Just as you get to your car door, he's in your face with a map asking for directions. The minute you stop to help him, another man inside the van opens the side doors, the man that's in your face, grabs you and put his hand with a cloth around your mouth and nose, then boom, you're out cold from the drug inside the cloth. There are many reasons why some men want to get in your face. You could be an easy target to rob or easily misled into doing what they ask of you. Some of these men will look to see how naïve you are before doing their thing. As silly as it may sound, some women do conduct themselves in ways that will make a man think they are truly naïve around men. Women who allow men to invade their space and put their hands on their shoulders are telling them that it's okay to conduct yourself with me this way.

They will not back down when they feel they are on a roll; before you know it, you too will get caught up in the frenzy and will start touching him. This exciting behavior could cause you to end up in the back seat of his car having sex or in a side room at a party making out. One thing will lead to another when your space is being invaded; after it's over, you may become very sorry for letting yourself get out of hand. Ladies, I keep saying that you are targets of pleasure for men who see you as a bowl of molten lust for a good time. Thousands of babies are being born every day because of the behavior of men who get their rocks off in a woman after invading her space and then go their way without looking back. This is what I meant when I said that these men are looking for naïve women who are easy-going. To the women who were raised better than this, I do hope your blinders are off and you can now see the big picture of what in your face is all about.

Men with these types of behaviors have many different types of professions and personalities. Don't let their professional status make you think they would never act this way. If one of our past presidents was able to go around grabbing women's crouches, then have the nerve to brag about it to his friends, what does that tell you about any man who may have that same mindset. Keep in mind, ladies, if you don't maintain control over your surrounding space, a disrespectful man will do it for you from the inside of your personal space. Friendly men are not always just being friendly; many of them have an ulterior motive for doing so. Some of the motives could be related to business or wanting to build a relationship with you. Whichever be the case, you need to keep your eyes open to fully understand what he's up to and where is he trying to go in wanting to get close to you. When he sees you're alert with many questions and on top of what he's trying to do, he may back down if he's up to no good. Educating yourself about men is the key to moving forward; unhindered by the greed and lust they have.

Chapter 16

BARE-FINGERED AND UNFAITHFUL

Many good women have run into men who claim to be single only to find out later they are married. Some of you might wonder why a man would do such a thing to his wife. Good question, and I will do my best to give you the answers you need to hear. First of all, when two people join together and are truly in love with each other; nothing should come between them if they are married. However, that is not always the case in relationships. Women who don't fully understand the man's needs can cause him to look elsewhere. We all know that the body of a woman is day-and-night different from a man, which means they each function in a different way. However, the sex drive is caused by the hormones they produce. The primary female sex hormones are estrogen and progesterone and men's primary sex hormone is testosterone. However, women do produce small amounts of this as well. Similarly, men also produce small amounts of estrogen and progesterone. These hormones, which are controlled by the brain, create the desire for sex.

Without getting too deeply into the medical aspects of what drives people into wanting to have sex; I'll stop with the hormones of both parties. Something that I have witnessed over the years with women is that they don't seem to have as much desire for sex as men do. It appears to me that men have a much stronger drive for sex than women. Some men can look at a woman and have an erection due to their desire and hormone buildup. A man with a sex drive like this can find it hard being married to a woman who doesn't fully understand his needs and desires. Some women can go through life never having a desire to be satisfied sexually. That is not to say that women don't have the desire; on the contrary, they do, but not in the same way as men. If you're a woman who's gone through menopause, you have another reason to keep having sex. Without regular intercourse, your vagina can tighten and its tissues can get thinner and be more likely to get injured, tear, or even bleed during sex. This can be so uncomfortable that women with these symptoms avoid having sex, which can make it worse.

Changes related to menopause, such as vaginal dryness and irritation, can be treated with lubricants, moisturizers, or low-dose estrogen. Regular sex helps you feel emotionally close to your partner, which opens the door to better communication. Couples who have sex more often tend to say they're happier than those who get less of it. However, it doesn't have to happen every day; once a week seems to be enough. This seems to be true no matter your age or gender or how long you've been in the relationship. This takes us back to better understanding the man's behavior when it comes to sex; they do have a stronger sex drive than most women. You very seldom hear of a woman raping a man—a boy maybe, but not a man. A man who finds himself horny and unable to get the satisfaction needed to calm himself down can become very unruly. His unsettled satisfaction can cause increased anxiety, depression, trouble sleeping at night, medical health problems due to not releasing himself, and wild imaginings.

"Wild imaginings?" you might ask. Yes, that's right, some women will hold back giving their husbands sex when they get angry at them. A woman who treats her husband like this over a long period can create multiple problems in the relationship. Most men will not force their wives to sleep with them, especially when they are hard up to be satisfied. Some of these men will think about Sally down the street and imagine being in bed with her. If the rejection from you continues over many days, he just may take a detour on the way home after work one day to stop at a club or bar far away from home, take off the wedding ring, and make himself comfortable around all the single ladies inside. Ladies, this is just one example of what some men will do to get the satisfaction you are not giving them. It's one thing to be on your period and or not feeling well or just not in the mood. When you have a legitimate reason for not satisfying your husband sexually, you need to communicate that to him with love and understanding. All of the things mentioned above about what happens to men when they are not satisfied sexually can be solved when you understand that their sexual needs are much stronger than yours.

Ladies, if you ever run into a man who has no ring on his finger and you're in conversation with him, ask him straight out, "How's your wife and kids doing?" You're giving him an open-ended question that must have two answers: Does he have a wife and does he have any kids. A slow answer and looking down or looking in any direction may be signs of guilt. The man who will lie to you is desperate for sexual satisfaction and will say anything to gain your trust. The sad part of this is that many naïve women will fall for his story and will later build a relationship with him. Your relationship with him could be a one- to two-hour drive from his family home, where his wife and/or children may be living. He may tell you he works out of town and you may see him only once a week or every two weeks. Whatever excuse you hear, you need to keep in mind that you are just a sidekick when his wife refuses to take care of his sexual needs at home. Over time, you may fall in love with the guy and, when you do find out he's married, many of you will still want to hang on to him.

This is how good women get trashed by devious and corrupt-minded men who will stop at nothing to get what they want. Relationships are nowhere close to what they used to be; people are not living together out of love, they are together out of lust and desires toward each other. Communicating with true love, concerns, and understanding has been put on the back burner by many couples. When problems hit the fan, instead of looking for counsel in a private setting, people are going on live TV, sharing their dirty laundry for the whole world to see and hear. Ladies, if you truly love your man, you need to fully understand his sexual needs and desires. If you now know by reading this book what happens when you fail to satisfy him sexually, step up and make it happen. If you don't feel like being penetrated by him, there are other ways you can take care of his needs. The bottom line is this: You don't want him taking off his ring; to look elsewhere for satisfaction.

There are a lot of good men who want to be true and faithful to their wives. However, when there is no clear communication and total rejection from you in giving them the love they deserve, it will be just a matter of time before many of them stop being faithful to you. Most women who are in good relationships have many of the attributes that Delilah had with Samson. They have a man who is truly in love with them and is willing to do anything to make them happy. In knowing this, some women will use their bodies to tease their husbands into getting them to do the things they want without proper communication. Ladies, unlike the Bible days, some of these men today can have short patience with you; their hormones will cause them to see that the grass on the other side of the fence is much greener. The key to a good relationship is good communication, understanding each other's needs, compromising on disagreements, and saying and showing how much you love each other through your actions when being together. This will help eliminate the unfaithful behaviors when you are in full support of each other's needs.

Chapter 17

AFTER VOWS ARE MADE
AND THE DOOR IS SHUT

M en and women can be unpredictable in relationships. However, our focus for this chapter
will be on the changing behavior of the man
after marriage. Meeting someone you like and later fall in
love with can be fun and exciting, although it would be
better for everyone to give themselves plenty of time for
checking out the person they feel most comfortable with. It
would save a lot of heartache and pain in the long run. The
other day, I took a break from my writing to watch a docu-
mentary about small monkeys roaming the streets in India.
It showed how some of the people sitting on benches in a
park were feeding the monkeys from bags of food. Every
now and then a monkey would come up to a person very
calmly and sit, waiting for that person to give them something to eat. I saw on many occasions those same monkeys
who were calm, patient, and waiting for the right moment
jerk the bag from the person's hand and run with it. Some
of the men I will be talking about have some of that same
behavior when dating women.

There are so many good and loving women looking for
Mr. Right, it is hard to tell if he really is, even after dating
for long periods of time. Like the monkeys, some of the

men will stay as long as it takes to get into your crotch; after they've got their fill of pleasure; they run away with your love in a bag. Then there are those who will stay for the long haul of dating because they plan to keep you for serving their daily needs in the future. They may tell you how much they love you, and some may really do, and they may later ask for your hand in marriage. If the relationship has been a short one, you should put the brakes on and think about how much time you've had in getting to know him. However, some quick marriages can turn out very well over the long haul. In these cases, the couples were obviously madly in love with each other. It doesn't always turn out that way for others, who pop the gun without taking their time. A man can be a wolf in sheep's clothing for a long or a short period. The way to know this is by watching everything about him throughout the dating period. In doing this, you could save yourself from the abuse you may suffer later if you see signs of strange behaviors, bad attitudes, and a quick temper.

In today's society, most couples want to do a test run before locking into each other's arms. Ladies, living together would not be a good idea, knowing that you could have babies in the short run. Living together doesn't always give you the full picture of what that man is capable of. If you both know that either of you can walk away from the relationship at any time, why take that chance to possibly get pregnant living together? Once this happens, you will find yourself depending on him more than you can imagine. Once he sees he has you in his clutches, he may start being himself, instead of who you thought he was. Once those doors open, your life will never be the same. Having children out of wedlock can possibly put more children into poverty situations. The man who may talk you into living with him may not see that child as his full responsibility to take care of.

The situation could go from bad to worse; the money that it took to take care of two people is now spread out for three people. An unexpected child coming on the scene creates tension, stress, and anger when two people are not in agreement on how to deal with the issues. The invisible and untrue vows you made by living together have now become your worst nightmare.

When true vows are made between hands of marriage, both parties are aware of the commitment they are making to each other. You become locked in a moral and value commitment, one that you hope will continue until the day you die. However, it doesn't always turn out that way; attitudes and behaviors tend to get rocky over periods of time. There are many reasons for this. My solution to some of these problems is to get counseling before marriage. I have performed several marriage ceremonies and, before each one, they had to spend at least two hours in full counseling with me. The purpose of this is to help the couple better understand what to expect within a marriage. They are briefed on the good times and the bad times and how to solve problems with positive communication between each other.

When the situation gets too hard for them to solve

themselves, they are to seek outside counseling to get back on track. When couples are counseled before marriage, the chances of them falling apart is low. Ladies, most men do not want to receive counseling before marriage. Some of these men already know how they are going to treat you and they resent being counseled on the right way to love and treat you in marriage. You may not believe this but, as I was working on this chapter of this book, I received a phone call from a guy wanting me to perform the marriage ceremony for him and his girlfriend. When I explained the process that he and his girlfriend had to go through before I would perform the wedding, he told me that it was not necessary because he had been married before. But she had never been married and, even if she had, they both would still have to attend marriage counseling before I would perform any ceremony. He rejected and ended up calling someone else to give him what he wanted.

Ladies, if you're a woman serious about living a good and righteous life with a future husband and before God, demand the right type of counseling with the man you're willing to settle down with. Don't just leave it up to him to decide your future life with him; the counseling will help you better understand what his responsibility is to you as his wife. When you come into this knowledge, it will then be easier for you to hold him accountable for his bad behavior toward you. Women who fail to get the proper counseling before marriage may not be able to see the true right and wrong that takes place at times. You might ask, "Doc, why is that so important?" I have counseled many women who have been beaten and abused by their husbands or boyfriends. The biggest problem I found in what they shared with me is this: Many of them thought it was their fault and they had to be punished for what they did. These women had been abused for so long that they had been made to believe that this is what marriage was all about: When you get in trouble, you have to be punished like a child to get it right.

Some of these men may have had fathers who would beat and verbally abuse their moms day in and day out. After becoming grown men, they may look back on their past and decide to be different and better husbands toward their wives. However, when their anger kicks in, many find themselves acting like their fathers toward their moms. That is why I keep saying that counseling before marriage will open your heart and mind to a better level of understanding. You good women need to be educated on how that man is supposed to treat you. When you have this knowledge, you become free of being ignorant about his monstrous behavior. You would then know where to draw the line concerning his abusive attitude and physical threats toward you. It takes two people to get married and it takes two people to make a baby. If one of the two decides not to move forward, what do you think the other person will do? Ladies, you do have a right to reject anything or anyone that may create problems in your life down the road. Don't tie the knot without good counseling; reject him if he refuses.

Chapter 18

DO WHAT I SAY OR GET BEATEN

D o what I say or get beaten; these are men who have no respect for women. They see women as pleasure providers, along with other things they would have them do. These are men who will knock a woman to the floor if she looks at them the wrong way. There are many different reasons for their sporadic behavior; much of it takes place behind closed doors. This is how some of these men will traumatize a woman into submitting to do their will only. There are many professional women, college students, high school students, and hard-working women who are in these situations right now. Some of them were kidnapped against their will and are locked up, unable to get the help they need. This type of torture can break any woman into surrendering to do whatever that man wants, without question.

Throughout this country and around the world, these women are locked up in places far and near. She could be your neighbor next door, whom you only see when he's at home. She could be held fifty miles out of town, in a two-bedroom house in a wooded area away from the population. There are many ways and places these women are being held. The problem is this: They are so mesmerized and afraid of being beaten again and again, or possibly being killed, that they will not say anything to anyone about their situation. As you read this, you may find it hard to think that women in situations like this would not say anything if they could.

People may not see it in the news very much but, trust me, when they do, it's hard for the average person to fathom what that woman went through. I don't care what others may say about the creation of man, this I do know: Some of them are the most corrupted and evil-minded creatures on the planet. The very people who are needed to populate the planet are being treated worse than animals. Ladies, most of you are such a joy to be around that I hope this will open your eyes to the reality of what some of these men can do to you. Mothers who failed to teach their daughters about the behaviors of these kinds of men have lost them to tragic death like this. It does not have to be this way; what you don't know can and will, in many cases, hurt you; and, in some cases, kill you. We've all heard the saying, "Knowledge is power." Well, I am sharing this knowledge with you to open your eyes to the reality of mankind. As a man, I have come into the knowledge of how they think by the work I've been doing as a counselor for so many years.

A person learning how to drive for the first time gives full attention to what is being said by the instructor. While on the road, that person is very vigilant to the things in front, on both sides, and periodically behind as well. Most drivers continue to operate that same way each time they get into their vehicle. Doc, why are you telling us this? Staying alert is one of the keys to driving any vehicle each time you get into your car to drive; you should do the same in dating men, being around them; and watching their behaviors. Remember what I shared with you above: Most of these men will be on their best behavior while in public places. When they think they have gained your trust, and feel that you have dropped your guard, that is when some of them will pull you into the corner of their deranged secret world. Make no mistake, ladies, you could be a nun walking down the street. These men have no respect for persons; what they would do to a nun is the same thing they would do to you if they catch you not paying attention to details.

"Doc, it sounds like you hate men." No, I don't, I just hate the way some of them treat women. Men who act this way are COWARDS in every way. The average woman cannot fight off a full-size man; she will get beaten down every time. Men like this will not attack someone comparable to themselves in size, so they prey on helpless women to get their thrills about how macho they are. Some of you may have a family member who is married to a monster like this. You may have tried many times in talking to her about leaving, but you see she's too afraid to do so. When you talk to her in private, she makes it seems like everything is okay and there's nothing to worry about. A woman who will act this way may be trying to protect you from his threats to harm you if she follows your recommendation. These men will make your sister, cousin, friend, or daughter believe that if any of their family members get involved in their business; they will be killed.

They will make her believe that she would be responsible for any of their deaths if she tries to leave him because of their concerns. A woman like this is so brainwashed by threats of harm and danger to others that she becomes a complete zombie walking in life. They have no joy, no real smile, no social life of any kind, and they evade their family and friends. How often do we see in the news that a man kills his wife and children or a man kills his wife and her mom and dad? The list could go on and on with crimes that have been committed against women and their families. How do you prevent this from happening? One way is to follow my instructions throughout this book and, when you see the first signs of violence being made toward you, get out of the relationship early. Once the pattern of negative behavior starts to form, it will later become the norm for dealing with problems. It will get worse and worse as time passes. That is why you should get out of that marriage or relationship at the first signs of physical violence toward you. Don't be a punching bag for any man who claims to love you.

Chapter 19

OVERCOMING YOUR FEARS

Sometimes fear stems from real threats, but it can also originate from imagined dangers. The question is, how do you overcome something that has not happened yet, and what do you think is generating this fear? The fear we all face is programmed into the nervous system and works like an instinct. From the time we're infants, we are equipped with the survival instincts necessary to respond with fear when we sense danger or feel unsafe. Fear helps protect us. It makes us alert to danger and prepares us to deal with it. Based on my knowledge of how some people see themselves, they can be the greatest threat of fear to themselves. You might ask, "How can that be?" Lack of confidence, low self-esteem, and fear of the unknown can cause women and men not to move forward in life. Being threatened by another person will deepen the levels of fear. The fear they already have within themselves and the outside threats will cause them to become paralyzed and unstable. This is one of the key reasons why so many women in abusive relationships fail to leave their abusers.

Regardless of what type of danger you face in life, once you overcome your fears, it then becomes easier to deal with the threats in front of you. Life is precious and should be enjoyed daily; if you truly love yourself and the life that has been given you; the desire to live on should be great. There is so much to live for and so much to enjoy, why let someone else try to take that away from you? This is where the instinct to live kicks in, in a very big way. The motivation you have for life will cause you to fight to the very end to survive. In my leisure time, I enjoy watching nature at its finest. I especially like watching the lions chase after other animals for food. Why? It shows me the strong determination the prey animals have to live. When they see the lions coming, they take off like speeding bullets; even after they are caught, they still put up a fight, to the very end of life. If the animals in the wild show this type of determination to live, do you not think that we, as human beings, should have that same instinct to do the same? Overcoming your fear determines how much you want to live. I am not saying you should not be afraid; on the contrary, that fear should be your motivation to fight for your independence and the right to be victorious in the end.

I have never seen an animal stand still watching a lion chasing after them; they do what comes naturally to them: RUN! Ladies, we as humans have better skills than the animals in the jungle. We don't have to run like them; we do, however, have ways to defeat the adversary who is trying to destroy us. The thing you have to keep in mind is: How much do you want to live? You may suffer pain for a little while, but that pain should be motivation enough for you to fight back, if you truly love life and yourself. The greatest motivator you have is the one that lives within you. Who is that you ask? Jesus Christ, Who is waiting on you to let go and let Him guide you through the process. You much believe in His awesome powers and the things He can do to bring you out of your misery. He will give you the boldness to stand, he will give you directions on what to do and how to free yourself from a bad situation. If you put your faith in Him, you will be able to do all things, through Him who strengthens you. However, you also must have faith in yourself for Him to work within you.

Remember the Bible story of Daniel in the lion's den? Daniel was a young man who put all his trust in God, the Father of all creation. He was a man who feared and loved God with all his heart and all his soul. During that time Israel was under the leadership of King Darius. A royal statue was made of him and everyone in the country had to bow down to worship it. This idea came from Daniel's enemies, who were very jealous that the king had made him second in charge of the kingdom. Daniel was humble, true, and faithful in the work that he did under the king's leadership. However, Daniel put all his faith in God, because he knew that nothing under God's creation could be more powerful than Him. When King Darius agreed to have the statue built, he did not know that those men under Daniel's leadership wanted to destroy him. He thought everyone agreed with the statue being made. Anyone not bowing down to worship it would be thrown into the lion's den. Although Daniel knew this, he never allowed himself to bow down to idle gods.

One evening, Daniel's enemies came by his house and watched through his window to see that he would pray three times a day to God the Father, Who created all things. His enemies went back and told King Darius what Daniel was doing. This king was surprised and depressed to hear that his leading man was not following the rules. He was pressed by other leaders to make Daniel pay the price that was decreed as punishment. Daniel was brought before the king and questioned about why he was doing this. Daniel gave his reasons and said that there was only one true God that he would bow down to, the God of all creation. The king himself loved Daniel enough to hope that his God would save him while in the lion's den. The king was unable to sleep that night because he was thinking about Daniel. The next day he went to see if Daniel was still alive. After reaching the den, he said, "O Daniel, servant of the living God, whom thou servest continually, was He able to deliver thee from the lions?" Daniel said to him, "O king, live forever; my God hath sent His angel, and hath shut the lions' mouths." Read Daniel 6:1

The faith that Daniel had in the God of all creation brought him through the most terrifying moments a person could deal with. Ladies, you don't have to be thrown into a lion's den to be saved from your enemies. Even with the smallest faith, God can take you out of the worst of the worst situations. The world we live in is full of evil men like the ones who tried to destroy Daniel. God sees your heart and He knows how faithful you are when you put your trust in Him. Lean not unto your own understanding on how to deal with small-minded men who see you as having little to no value in life. God will give you wisdom, knowledge, and understanding of how to deal with people like this. That's why it is important for you to put your trust and faith in Him; He will get you through the perils of life. Overcoming your fears is knowing that you have a source of power that only God controls.

Chapter 20

THE VALUE YOU SEE IN YOURSELF

I f mankind could see the true value they hold within themselves, they might be encouraged to change from their negative ways toward other people. It will give them a better outcome when God determines their worth in the end. Each of our lives has an eternal soul that will truly answer before God for the horrible things we do to others. Ladies, you may be the weaker vessel among men but you still have a soul that will answer before God for your lack of faith and unbelief in Him. How you value yourself in this world will determine how God (if He allows you to enter into His Kingdom) will value you. What do I mean by "If He lets you in?" Good question; everybody that's talking about going to heaven may not be going there. Many of them will be heading in the opposite direction to eternal punishment for the deeds they did on planet earth.

I did say in an earlier chapter that man was the most corrupt-minded creature on the planet. Ladies, regardless of where you find yourself in life or the situation you may be in, man cannot save you from what is to come nor can you save yourself. When you cross from this life to the eternal life or the eternal dying death to come, it will be because you truly had a personal relationship with God, through Christ Jesus His Son, who is the only One that can save you, or with the prince of darkness, satan, the evil of this world. One of the two relationships will determine the direction you will go. The evil of this world is run by satan, the father of all lies. The good is through Jesus Christ the Son of God, Who was also God in the flesh. He gave His life to save you from going to the same place where satan will spend eternity. The world we live in may be corrupt but our God sees a lot of good in us to save us from ourselves. We have all been given free will to make decisions in moving forward at whatever we chose to do in life.

Everything we do is based on the decisions we make ourselves and is also influenced by two spirits, the spirit of evil and the spirit of righteousness. To stay on track in doing the right thing, you need to have a better understanding of how God operates with His people. The way to do that is to read the King James Bible. This book alone, with the messages from men who were inspired by God, is sharing the truth of how God operates and can teach you His will for your life. Not all preachers and pastors in today's society are preaching the will of God to the people. Many are preaching to empty your pocketbooks to make themselves rich. This is why I keep saying that man is corrupt because many of them have no respect for God's truth. I am talking about jack-leg preachers who will rob you blind by making you think they are men of God. The Pharisees did the same thing when Jesus walked the earth; they lied to the people and took advantage of them during bad times.

Regardless of how bad things may currently be in your life and the pain that is thrown on you under the rule of man, taking your own life would be a curse to yourself. The life we have been given is short but what comes with that life is what motivates us to live right. "What is that?" you may ask. Your eternal soul, because it will never perish. Those who fail to see the real value that is within them will suffer the greatest loss of that gift of life. Many years ago, there was a school shooting; several young boys had made up their minds to kill anyone who claimed to be a Christian. One of the boys grabbed a girl and asked her to deny her faith as a Christian, she refused, and he hatefully shot her in the head in front of other kids. Her faith in God at that moment of death gave her instant eternal life through Christ Jesus our Lord and Savior. She believed that God would save her from death and He did just that by taking her away from the pain and suffering in this world.

Ladies, no amount of pain you can suffer in this world should make you want to give up on life; it is the gateway to eternal freedom through Jesus Christ. The young girl in that school shooting made the right choice and that choice was to live forever. If you're a single woman looking for a man to love and respect you, that man should have the same Christian faith as you. Although you both may be of the same faith, you will still have problems between yourselves. As you grow in your relationship, your faith in God and your conscience will reveal the wrong you do to each other. It is a much better process than hooking up with someone who has no belief in God or His Son. This is where so many good women fall through the cracks; they hook up with a man who has no morals or values in life.

These are the ones that satan will use to destroy you day in and day out.

Don't let a man's charms, good looks, or sweet talk make you think he's the one. Find out what he believes in and what he values the most in life. These two questions, in part, will determine whether you two will be able to see eye to eye on certain issues within the relationship. If you know upfront that you're not going to be able to walk together down the same road of life's issues, why bother tying the knot with him? One of two things will happen; you may end up giving up your faith in God just to follow his undetermined direction in life. On the other hand, you may later regret ever meeting him because of his abusive behavior toward you. Men who live in this world without directions in life become part of the world and everything it has to offer. The negative things we learn in life teach us valuable lessons about not crossing that path again. That stands only for those who want to live a better life full of love and trust; those who don't care will repeat their mistakes over and over, again and again. Once you step onto his merry-go-round world, you might find it hard getting off on your own.

In the beginning, men were created to lead. However, it appears that many of them have fallen by the wayside. They were meant to set positive examples for women and children to have better lives, not suffer through hardship. Women who have taken the role of leadership around the world should continue setting the example for the men who have fallen. In today's society, women have to become mentally strong and prepared to overcome the weakness of the man they are with. That man might be your husband or boyfriend; either way, if he is not being the man that he is supposed to be, it would be a good idea for you to help him seek counseling to get him on the right track. You will not be disrespecting him in any way; you would be is taking the lead in helping him understand his bad, poor, or evil ways. If you don't take charge of the bad situation unfolding, you both will drown in pain, sorrow, confusion, and lack of trust in each other.

Chapter 21

FINDING GOOD MEN IN
THE RIGHT PLACES

It's not at all hard to find a good, respectful, and caring man; they are all around us. The problem with a lot of good women is that they seem to be looking in all the wrong places. "How so?" you might ask. I will give you some examples of places many of you go to look for a man. I will also tell you why it's not a good idea to be looking in these places. There are men of all types who like to hang out at bars, clubs, casinos, all-night dance clubs, and beer parties, to name a few. Do you wonder what's wrong with that? I have found that many of these men, along with the women in these places, are unstable in their relationships. Many of them find it hard to slow down from the heavy partying to get serious about living a solid life with someone. Many grown men and women still have that teenage mentality of wanting to party all night and then go home drunk after spending all their money.

I am still working with couples who have these same problems. Husband will put his family on the back burner while spending the family's income at casinos, beer taverns, and club partying all night. Many married men hang out at these places without their wives knowing it. Many will claim to be single just to have you on the side for dating.

Dating a man like that in one of those places would be like throwing the dice and hoping you hit that lucky number. You could easily say that all the men in these places are not that way. Yes, you would be right in saying that. However, why would any good woman, knowing this, take the chance in looking in areas like that, when you know the risk of finding a good-for-nothing man is high. The risk you take in looking for a man in these areas can affect your unborn children. How? His unstable behavior, hardly ever being around when you would need him, possibly showing little financial support for the family, and being very abusive toward you and your kids when drunk. Women who accept finding men in these areas, in my opinion, are desperate to be in a relationship or are too naïve to see the big picture of what could happen down the road.

Women who are young and in college, you are in the right place for finding a man that is going places and is hoping to be something in life. This is one of the key areas for young women starting out. For women not in college who are available for dating, look for a man who is stable in a good profession. You may have friends who know good and respectable men who are single. Your church may have single men in leadership positions who may be hoping to find someone like you. Many churches have special gatherings for single men and women, hoping to find same-faith relationships. There are many other possible ways of finding good men; you just have to take your time and weed out the good from the bad. There are, however, things you need to know about dating men who are trying to be careful and respectable. They too get horny faster than you would and may try to get you in bed a night or two later. That is the natural part of that man; you just have to be strong for yourself and not let him cause you to make the wrong decision.

Many couples who start dating truly want to spend time getting to know each other on a better level. However, too often they make the mistake of giving in to each other before a true commitment is made. When you become pregnant and you tell him, one of two things will happen. He will get excited and want to get married before the child is born, or he might disappear and you'll never find him again. These are situations that start right but you dropped your guard and allowed him to come into you. Being pressured by your boyfriend to have sex should be discussed between you and him. You should ask him questions about the what-ifs and, if you do get pregnant, what will he do? I talked about how you value yourself in an earlier chapter; well, the time to do so is in situations like this. Cutting yourself short for a fun night in bed with him can cause you years and years of pain and sorrow and could be a mistake that you regret making after looking back on it.

Much of finding a good man really depends on you, the woman. If you truly value yourself and want to be respected by the man you are dating, you much take charge of your body and your own lustful thoughts. If you both find it hard to resist each other sexually when together, you as the woman should take a step back and look at yourself. Take a time out to reexamine what you're doing; and where it's leading you. You should not only look at yourself but also at how you feel about him and how he really feels about you. You should ask if he's the right guy for the long haul or if he's just a good-time friend. People who have been friends for many years tend to think they know each other well. That may be true on the outside of knowing that person but getting involved romantically will show a different side of that person over time.

There are friendship relationships that have worked out quite well over the long haul. However, many of them can be very disappointing over a short period. Just when you think you know someone, it's not until you are living with them that you see who that person really is and what they are all about. There is only one friend that I know of who will never disappoint you. He's a friend above all the friends you'll ever have in life; his name is Jesus. He's been my friend through thick and thin, ups and downs, pain and sorrow, and the good and bad times. Ladies, if you are having a difficult time finding the right man, my friend, who can be your friend as well, will help you in your journey. He knows better than you who would be the right man for you. You just need to put your trust in Him to help you meet the right man. Don't let your lustful thoughts speak for you; follow your heart and ask Jesus to help you make the right decisions in finding the right man.

Pray to Him, and ask Him to give you wisdom, knowledge, and understanding in all that you do in life. At the same time, you should acknowledge Him in all your ways. In doing this, you are putting Him in the driver's seat of everything you do in life. If you can't give my friend Jesus the same love, respect, and support He's giving you when you need it, then you cannot expect Him to rush to your calls when you need Him the most. Ignoring Him and leaning on your own thoughts can and will get you in trouble when the wrong choices in life are made. The relationship you should have with Him is that of a spiritual nature. He sees everything you do; He knows your thoughts before you think them. Therefore, you should be aware of His presence around you at all times. He will never give you the wrong answer to any decisions you make in life. He loves you more than you love yourself and that, my lady friend, speaks volumes about the trust you should have in Him.

One of the hardest things for men and women to do when they don't have a strong relationship with Jesus is to put their faith in Him. Why? Because faith is believing in something or someone whom you have not seen yet. Many people walk by the sight of what they see each day. When they need something, if they can't see a way to get it, they'll leave it alone or get it the wrong way. *Faith is the substance of things hoped for; and the evidence of things not yet seen.* (Hebrews 11:1 KJB) Ladies, the man you want and the man you are having a difficult time finding is waiting for you. You just have not met or seen him yet but, when you put your faith in Jesus our Lord and Savior, He will direct your path to him. This is what faith is all about, putting your trust in Him; He will never let you down.

Chapter 22

CLOSING WORDS AND THOUGHTS

Ladies, throughout Section II of this book, I've tried to fill you with the understanding of what men are all about. I have given you the ins and outs of how many of them see you and how they think about you as a woman. If your eyes are not open to what you've been reading in this book, it's because you've accepted their behavior and are willing to submit to their terms. It does not have to be that way for any of you if you follow the instructions that have been given to be successful. Doors will open only if you believe in yourself and in the higher power that is within you. We have all heard the saying that you can lead a horse to water, but you can't make him drink. The same is true for all human beings. You can be taught the truth and the righteousness of life but you can't be made to live the life that is righteous and pleasing before God. You have to want the good of what life has to offer. Rushing in with both legs, both hands, mouth, and crotch may only create pain and sorrow later on in life. We live in a world full of lust and temptation, which makes it hard for the average man and woman to move forward in doing the right thing.

Why is that? The flesh is weak in all human beings but the spirit of righteousness is willing to do right if we surrender to it. Our bodies are nothing more than lumps of clay, yet in each of us, is a soul that will be judged by God. Out fleshly body houses that soul, which allows the spirit of God to communicate with you day in and day out. Each time you surrender to the temptations of this world, you are ignoring the righteous communications from God through His spirit, which is telling you to refrain from your sinful nature. Of course, that's easier said than done when you're not connected to His will for your life. What do I mean by that? Good question; each time you get into your car to go somewhere and you know the battery is not connected; what do you think you will have to do to get it going? That's right, open the hood to connect it. Common sense will tell you to keep the battery connected to the cables under the car hood at all times. That way you will not have to go through the trouble of getting dirty, trying to connect every time you leave your house.

The metaphor of the car above is the same process in staying connected with the spirit of God through his son Jesus. He stays connected with you throughout the day and night. That is the purpose of the Holy Spirit living within your soul. Your soul says "Yes" to God's will, but your fleshly body is saying "Yes" to the temptations of this world. What has taken place within you is spiritual warfare between you, the evil spirit of satan, and the spirit of righteousness through Jesus Christ our Lord and Savior. It is a never-ending battle in the life we live each day. That is why it is so important for you to acknowledge Him in all your ways. If you fail to do this, you will surely disconnect from His will for your life. Things may go well while you're disconnected and you may go through each day never taking the time to thank Him for all his goodness and mercy. Failing to acknowledge Him in your daily living is like saying, "I don't need You right now; I'll call on You when I'm in trouble."

The problem with that is this: If you're not willing to acknowledge Him in your daily living, He may not be there when you are in dire need of help and you have no one to turn to. Prayer is the key, faith unlocks doors, and staying connected will keep you on the right track in life. For those of you who are young and fairly new to life's disappointing moments, I hope this book will open your eyes to the reality of life. If you're a woman who has been in the playing field for many years and you are nearly at the end of your rope; now is the time to call out His name, repent of your sinful nature, surrender yourself to His will. In doing this, you will be taking the weight of the world off your shoulders. When you put all your faith in man, you can become stressed out, worried about everything and nothing, they can cause you to have anxiety attacks, become depressed, and lose patients. Having Jesus in your life will give you the freedom to live your life worry-free. Why? Because you would be turning all your problems over to Him; you're putting Him in control. He is your source of strength and power. Greater is He that is within you than the men of this world that will destroy you, day in and day out.

Ladies, time is not on your side; it never will be in this world. Every day is a new opportunity to take charge of who you are and where you want to be in life. There is no guarantee of tomorrow nor OF the next breath of air you breathe. Putting off today for tomorrow may be too late for some of you. Our souls will have to answer for every dirty deed we did in this life. However, all of that can be washed away by repenting and letting Jesus be the real man in your life. That is not to say that you can't have an earthly man; on the contrary, Jesus came to save you from yourself and from all the danger that will lead you in the wrong direction. Mankind is of a sinful nature and cannot save you, neither can he save himself. It is up to you to follow the right path to eternal life through Christ Jesus. You do this through prayer, fasting, meditating on His words of truth, and staying connected by the faith you have in Him. He will never steer you wrong and, whatever trials you go through in life, if you hold on to His unchanging hand, you will be rewarded in the end in ways you could never imagine.

Another Book Title by Dr. Isaac O'Quin
Published by Tate Publishing, LLC.
And republished by Yorkshire Publishing

Breaking Through Poverty with a Spiritual Heart: by Isaac O'Quin.

This book can be ordered from the BTPWASH Christian Ministries Website, located at: www.btpwash.com

Isaac O'Quin is available to conduct seminars on this and other topics. He can be reached via e-mail at: Counseling@btpwash.com or btpwash@gmail.com or by phone: 253-216-4598 or 360-480-0656

Additional Resources by Other Authors

Banks, Bill & Sue. *Breaking Unhealthy Soul-Ties*

Virkler, Mark & Patti. *Prayers That Heal the Heart:*

Booker, Richard. *Seated in Heavenly Places*

Murray, Andrew. *Abide in Christ*

Slagle, Charles. *From the Father's Heart*

Virkler, Mark & Patti. *Counseled By God*

Bennett, Rita. *Emotionally Free*

Virkler, Mark & Patti. *Dialogue with God*

Tozer, A. W. *The Pursuit of Man*

Prince, Derek. *Blessing or Curse*

Hammond, Frank & Ida Mae. *Pigs in the Parlor*

Virkler, Mark & Patti. *Am I Being Deceived?*

Torrey, R. A. *The Person & Work of the Holy Spirit*

CPSIA information can be obtained
at www.ICGtesting.com
Printed in the USA
LVHW111928131221
705881LV00017B/121